MW00414628

SNAP
REVISION

THE CURIOUS INCIDENT OF THE DOG IN THE NIGHT-TIME

AQA GCSE English Literature

NIKKI
SMITH

REVISE SET TEXTS
IN A SNAP

Published by Collins
An imprint of HarperCollinsPublishers
1 London Bridge Street,
London, SE1 9GF

© HarperCollinsPublishers Limited 2017

9780008247157

First published 2017

10 9 8 7 6 5 4 3 2

British Library Cataloguing in Publication Data.

A CIP record of this book is available from the
British Library.

Printed in the UK by Martins the Printer Ltd.

Commissioning Editor: Gillian Bowman
Managing Editor: Craig Balfour
Author: Nikki Smith
Copyeditor: David Christie
Proofreaders: Jill Laidlaw and Louise Robb
Project management and typesetting:
  Mark Steward
Cover designers: Kneath Associates and
  Sarah Duxbury
Production: Natalia Rebow

ACKNOWLEDGEMENTS
Quotations from *The Curious Incident of the
Dog in the Night-Time (play)* by Mark Haddon;
adapted by Simon Stephens © Mark Haddon
and Simon Stephens, 24 July 2012, *The Curious
Incident of the Dog in the Night-Time (Modern
Plays)*, Bloomsbury Methuen Drama, an imprint of
Bloomsbury Publishing Plc.

The author and publisher are grateful to the
copyright holders for permission to use quoted
materials and images.

Every effort has been made to trace copyright
holders and obtain their permission for the use of
copyright material. The author and publisher will
gladly receive information enabling them to rectify
any error or omission in subsequent editions. All
facts are correct at time of going to press.

Contents

Part One: Finding the Dog

You must be able to: tell the difference between present and past events.

The setting

The play opens in the garden of a neighbouring house on Christopher's street in Swindon. It is seven minutes past midnight.

After finding a dead dog, Christopher is taken to the police station. Other than this, Christopher does not leave the neighbourhood in Part One of the play. He goes to school but it is clear that he does not venture far from home most of the time.

What is the situation?

Christopher has discovered a neighbour's dog, Wellington, which has been killed with a garden fork. Mrs Shears is the owner of the dog and she thinks that Christopher has killed it, although this is not the case.

When the police arrive to investigate, Christopher gets stressed and hits an officer who tries to handle him by taking his arm. Christopher is arrested and his father is required to pick him up from the police station.

Christopher likes dogs and starts a project to find out who killed Wellington, although his father has told him not to.

Who are the main characters?

Christopher is the main character of the play. He has a pet rat, Toby, and likes science and maths.

He lives with his father, Ed, and has been told that his mother died of a heart attack two years ago.

Christopher's teacher is Siobhan and she is helping him write his story about discovering the dead dog. Siobhan acts as a **narrator**, reading parts of Christopher's story aloud. This helps the audience learn important features of Christopher's life and the way that he thinks.

What do we learn about Christopher and his life?

Although it is never explicitly mentioned in the play, it is assumed that Christopher has a **developmental disability** called **Asperger syndrome**. When he gets stressed he uses a personal technique that he calls 'groaning' to calm himself down.

He likes to be **precise** and observes detailed facts in his story. He finds people confusing because he cannot understand their facial expressions or the meaning of language that is not direct, such as **metaphors**. He does not tell lies.

Christopher does not go to a mainstream school. He appears to have a good relationship with his school teacher, Siobhan, who helps him to understand the world and find ways to function appropriately in it.

Key Quotations to Learn

Christopher: 'The dog was dead.'

Christopher: 'It was seven minutes after midnight.'

Siobhan (speaking from Christopher's story): 'I find people confusing.'

Summary

- Christopher has found a neighbour's dead dog but nobody knows who killed it.
- Christopher's reactions to situations reveal his condition, the challenges it poses and the way he deals with it.
- Although Christopher's father has told him to keep his nose out of other people's business, he decides to find out who killed Wellington.
- Siobhan, who is helping Christopher write his story, reads a section that tells us about his mother's death.

Questions

QUICK TEST
1. How has Wellington been killed?
2. Why does Christopher decide to find out who killed Wellington?
3. What two reasons does Christopher give for finding people confusing?
4. What does Christopher think happened to his mother?
5. What is Christopher's relationship with Siobhan like?

EXAM PRACTICE
Using one or more of the 'Key Quotations to Learn', write a paragraph analysing how Stephens uses the events at the start of the play to help reveal aspects of Christopher's character.

Part One: Detecting

You must be able to: understand what Christopher learns through his detecting.

What do we learn from Christopher's investigations with his neighbours?

Christopher doesn't know many of his neighbours and they don't seem to know what is going on in the neighbourhood.

Mrs Alexander is an elderly lady who has a grandson close to Christopher's age and is friendly towards Christopher, inviting him in for some tea.

Christopher does not like strangers and people he is not familiar with so he will not go inside Mrs Alexander's house. He does agree to have a drink outside but gets nervous when she takes so long to bring it and walks away.

Christopher knows that the prime suspect in many murder cases is someone close to the victim. He concludes that Mr Shears killed Wellington as he was close to him. He also assumes that Mr Shears did not like Mrs Shears as he divorced her and so may have wanted to upset her.

When Ed finds out what Christopher has been doing he calls Mr Shears an 'evil man' and bans Christopher from carrying on with his **investigations**.

What else is going on in Christopher's life at this time?

Christopher's father, Ed, has challenged the school to allow Christopher to take his A-Level Maths exam.

The school feel that this is unusual practice and would set a precedent for other students to make specific requests.

Ed knows that Christopher is very good at maths and that since life presents so many other challenges for Christopher, he should be given this opportunity. He will not take no for an answer.

What else do we learn about Christopher's character?

He cannot understand the existence of heaven and God because, scientifically, there is no evidence for their location in the universe.

He does not like the colours yellow or brown and will not eat any yellow or brown coloured food. He does like the colours red and 'metal'.

He would like to be an astronaut because he knows he is intelligent enough and would enjoy the **solitary** nature of being in space. Sometimes he pretends he is in space by lying on his lawn to look at the stars.

He likes 'little spaces' and uses places such as the airing cupboard as a way of being alone and where he can think and feel calm.

What unexpected twist is presented at this point in the play?

Christopher's mother was having an affair with Mr Shears before she died.

Mrs Alexander told Christopher this because she was worried she had confused him by saying that his father, Ed, did not like Mr Shears.

Key Quotations to Learn

Stage directions: 'Mr Wise *laughs*. Christopher *walks away.*'

Ed: 'I'm not going to take no for an answer.'

Mrs Alexander: 'I'm not a stranger, Christopher, I'm a friend. '

Rhodri: 'God you do get the third degree, don't you?'

Summary

- Christopher approaches various neighbours on his street to find out information about who killed Wellington.
- Christopher concludes that Mr Shears is the prime suspect in the murder.
- Ed is not happy that Christopher has been investigating and forbids him from carrying on with his investigations.
- Mrs Alexander tells Christopher that his mother was having an affair with Mr Shears before she died. She thinks this is probably why Ed does not like Mr Shears.

Questions

QUICK TEST

1. What does Mrs Alexander know about Christopher before they meet?
2. Why does Christopher conclude Mr Shears is the prime suspect?
3. What, specifically, does Ed make Christopher promise?
4. What does Mrs Alexander not realise about what Christopher knows?

EXAM PRACTICE

Using one or more of the 'Key Quotations to Learn', write a paragraph analysing how other people respond to Christopher.

Part One: Finding the Letters

You must be able to: recognise the significance of the new discoveries Christopher makes.

What is the first reason why this part of the play is so shocking?

When Christopher's father finds Christopher's book, and reads what Mrs Alexander has told him, he is very angry. He shouts at Christopher, swears at him, is sarcastic about his Asperger's and eventually ends up in a physical fight that he starts by grabbing Christopher's arm.

He apologises to Christopher after he has had a drink. He tells him that he loves him and that he only loses his temper because he worries about Christopher.

Christopher tells Siobhan that this incident has not caused him to feel scared of his dad.

What is Christopher's unexpected discovery?

On trying to find his book that his father took after their fight, Christopher discovers a box with 43 letters from his mother addressed to him. They are post-marked after the date she was supposed to have died and have been sent from London. Christopher is confused at first but eventually he realises that his mother is still alive and is living with Mr Shears.

Why else do we feel shocked by Ed at this part of the play?

Not only did Ed lie to Christopher about his mother being dead but he has been hiding her attempts to contact Christopher ever since she moved.

What is his mother trying to communicate through the letters?

Judy explains that she found it hard to cope looking after Christopher. She always felt that Ed was more patient than she was and that he had a better relationship with Christopher.

Ed and Judy argued a lot and eventually stopped talking. She started spending time with Mr Shears because she felt so lonely. She did not want to hurt Christopher but felt that he would be better off if she was not living at home.

What is the final shock revealed at this part of the play?

Ed is very concerned when he discovers Christopher has read the letters. He is gentle with Christopher and says he did not mean to lie but he did not know how to explain the situation to him.

He wants Christopher to trust him and tells him that he killed Wellington. He did it because he was angry with Mrs Shears who rejected his desire to form a romantic relationship after Judy left.

How does Christopher respond to all this new information?

After Christopher reads the letters he is sick and curls into a small ball on the floor. He does not respond to his father or resist when he undresses him.

He starts groaning and counting once Ed has left so that he can think. He feels that it is not safe to stay at home with his father and decides to go to his mother's house in London.

Key Quotations to Learn

Siobhan: 'When I started writing my book there was only one mystery to solve.'

Ed: 'Come on, you're the memory man.'

Judy: 'I thought I was doing the best for all of us'

Siobhan (speaking from Christopher's story): 'I made a decision.'

Summary

- Ed finds Christopher's book and they get into a fight.
- He takes the book from Christopher but Christopher searches for it when Ed is out.
- Christopher finds letters written to him by his mother showing that she is still alive and living in London with Mr Shears.
- Christopher is sick and cannot respond when his father finds him.
- Ed wants Christopher to trust him and tells him the whole truth about the situation with Judy and Mrs Shears. He also tells him that he killed Wellington.
- Christopher feels that his father is dangerous and so he decides to go to his mother's house.

Questions

QUICK TEST
1. What did Judy dream her life would be like if she hadn't married Ed?
2. How did Christopher find the letters?
3. Why did Judy say that she had left home?
4. Who killed Wellington?
5. Why does Christopher reason that his father is dangerous?

EXAM PRACTICE
Using one or more of the 'Key Quotations to Learn', write a paragraph outlining the developing **tension** leading to the end of Part One of the play.

Part Two: Travelling to London

You must be able to: identify the degree of challenge facing Christopher on his journey to London.

Why is the journey to London so significant?

Christopher's journey to London is presented as a series of **trials**, many of which cause him significant stress. The extended **sequencing** of events necessary to travel, probably quite familiar and ordinary to the audience, allows them to experience with Christopher the degree of challenge he has to overcome.

Christopher uses **practical** methods of working out what to do and where to go. He imagines a red line on the ground in the direction he is walking and turns his footsteps into a **rhythm** that he can repeat in his mind to help him focus.

His success in overcoming each new problem presented, and his ability to thwart both Ed and the policeman's attempts to stop him, highlights his determination that he must leave home.

What causes Christopher stress on his way to London?

Christopher has never ventured this far from home alone before and he has not travelled on his own on a train so every part of the experience is new to him.

He is initially overwhelmed by all the sights and sounds of the train stations as he notices everything and struggles to read all the adverts and signs. Many people would just ignore all this unnecessary information but the audience are included in Christopher's experience through the **cacophony** of **pre-recorded** voices that ensures we are made aware of every single detail.

How does he manage his stress?

The new **environments** he finds himself in are very disordered but he makes order within them by creating rhythms and **patterns**. For example, the noise of the train approaching is overwhelming but he calms down by observing the pattern of: 'Train coming. Train stopped. Doors open. Train going. Silence'.

When he is walking through the station in London, Christopher makes his hand into a telescope to limit his field of vision so that he can concentrate on where he is going.

He feels protected by carrying his Swiss Army knife, which he shows to people as a warning to leave him alone. He also barks to warn people off.

On the train, he finds a small space behind some bags on the luggage rack which he can squeeze into and be alone.

He calms himself down by counting prime numbers.

Is Christopher completely successful?

Christopher achieves his **objective** of getting to his mother's house. However, while he shows **initiative** in doing so, his limited focus and inability to perceive wider **implications** means he is still quite vulnerable. On losing Toby, he climbs down onto the tracks of the tube unaware of the danger he is in, ignoring the protestations of people who try to help him back up again.

Key Quotations to Learn

Siobhan: 'And count the rhythm in your head because that helps, doesn't it?'

Stage directions: *'He barks at them like a dog.'*

Stage directions: *'For the first time he is alone on stage.'*

Information: 'Are you for real?'

Summary

- Christopher manages to get himself from Swindon to his mother's house in London by himself.
- He finds his way by creating rhythms and patterns in the surroundings.
- He is overwhelmed by the new sights and sounds he comes across.
- He calms himself down by using some of his Asperger's **coping mechanisms**.
- Ed has contacted the police and Christopher hides from an officer on the train.

Questions

QUICK TEST

1. How does Christopher find his way to the train station?
2. Why does the policeman end up travelling with Christopher?
3. How does Christopher shake him off?
4. How does he find out how to use the tube?
5. In what ways are the audience made to experience the challenge of Christopher's journey?

EXAM PRACTICE

Using one or more of the 'Key Quotations to Learn', write a paragraph explaining the challenges facing Christopher on this new journey and how he manages to deal with them.

Part Two: Meeting Judy

You must be able to: understand the impact on both Christopher and Judy caused by his arrival in London.

How does Judy react to Christopher's appearance in London?

Judy's response to Christopher's arrival could be felt as quite a shock to the audience – she appears to have forgotten that he does not like physical contact and tries to hug him.

She is pleased to see him, though, and is concerned to get him changed, cleaned and comfortable in her house.

She is extremely distressed to learn that Christopher thought that she was dead and she is very angry with Ed. She says she thought she may never see Christopher again as she never received a response to her letters.

What stress does Christopher's arrival in London cause for Judy?

Ed arrives to see Christopher on the first night but Christopher does not want to see him. Judy calls the police and they make Ed leave.

Judy's new partner, Roger (Mr Shears), does not seem very happy at having Christopher around; he is sarcastic and argumentative, making things even more difficult for Judy.

Judy loses her job as she does not go in for two days because she is looking after Christopher.

As Christopher struggles to deal with his new situation, he displays some of his old behaviours, such as walking down the street in the middle of the night, which cause Judy to worry. He also stops eating and she has to create a behaviour chart to encourage him with rewards.

Ed threatens to take Judy to court.

What is the issue with the maths exam?

Christopher is scheduled to be taking his Maths A-Level in Swindon shortly. He wants to return to do this but Judy does not think it is possible and calls his school to postpone it for a year, this makes Christopher very upset.

What is Roger's problem?

He says the flat is too small for three people and there is nowhere for Christopher to go to school.

He is sarcastic about Judy's management of Christopher and gets annoyed when Christopher doesn't want the books he has bought for him.

He does not seem very sympathetic to the feelings of either of Judy or Christopher, focussing more on the inconvenience Christopher's arrival creates for him. One night he gets drunk and shouts at Christopher and then tries to grab him.

Key Quotations to Learn

Stage directions: '*She starts to howl.*'

Ed: 'You were the one that bloody left.'

Judy: 'It's only an exam.'

Judy: 'I swear to God, Christopher, I love you but ...'

Roger: 'Well, it's nice to know my contribution is appreciated.'

Summary

- Christopher's arrival takes both Judy and Roger by surprise.
- Ed arrives at Judy's flat and they argue over each other's treatment of him.
- Christopher won't talk to Ed and Judy calls the police so Ed has to leave.
- Judy postpones Christopher's Maths A-Level, which upsets him.
- Christopher's presence causes stress and arguments between Judy and Roger.

Questions

QUICK TEST
1. What is Judy's reaction to hearing that Ed said she was dead?
2. Why does the police officer decide to leave Christopher with Judy?
3. Why can't Christopher sleep?
4. Why does Christopher not like the books Roger gets him?
5. Why is Roger angry with Christopher?

EXAM PRACTICE
Using one or more of the 'Key Quotations to Learn', write a paragraph examining the stress created by Christopher's arrival in London.

Part Two: Returning to Swindon

You must be able to: understand the ending to Christopher's story.

Why do Christopher and Judy go back to Swindon?

Judy and Christopher leave London in the middle of the night, taking Roger's car while he is asleep.

Judy says they need to do this because if they stayed someone was going to get hurt but that would not necessarily be Christopher.

It seems as though her relationship with Mr Shears is over.

How does Ed start to rebuild his relationship with Christopher?

Ed stays with Rhodri while Judy lives at home with Christopher and looks for somewhere more permanent to live.

Once they have moved to a bedsit, Christopher has to go to his father's house after school in the afternoons while his mother is at work. He shuts himself in his bedroom and pushes his bed up against the door in case his father tries to get in.

Eventually, Ed says they cannot carry on like this. He wants to rebuild Christopher's trust in him and creates a project for them to complete together; Christopher must learn to engage with his father again by using an egg timer to control the amount of time they spend together.

Ed buys Christopher a dog, which he calls Sandy. It stays at Ed's house and Christopher can spend time with it when he goes there.

What does Christopher achieve by the end of the play?

Christopher is agitated about being back in Swindon and not being able to do his A-Level Maths exam. His mother takes him into school and although he hasn't been sleeping very well, and hasn't had anything to eat, he sits the exam.

He has to use some counting techniques to calm himself down but he completes all the papers and gets an A*.

What are Christopher's plans for the future?

Christopher is now studying for his Further Maths A-Level. After that, he is going to sit his Physics A-Level and apply to university.

He has decided that he does not like London but he can apply to other universities in other big cities. He wants to live in a flat with Sandy.

He is aiming to get a first-class honours degree and then become a scientist.

He feels he can achieve all of this because he solved the mystery of Who Killed Wellington. In addition, he had to be brave in order to find his mother in London and he has written a book.

Key Quotations to Learn

Judy: 'We're going to the school.'

Ed: '... let's call it a project.'

Christopher: 'He's called Sandy.'

Christopher: 'Does that mean I can do anything, do you think?'

Summary

- Judy leaves Roger and takes Christopher back to Swindon.
- Christopher sits his Maths A-Level and gets an A*.
- Ed buys Christopher a dog that he calls Sandy.
- Ed and Christopher start to rebuild their relationship by spending small chunks of time with each other.
- Christopher decides that he wants to take more exams and go to university.

Questions

QUICK TEST

1. How does Judy explain that Ed is not likely to go to prison for killing Wellington?
2. What is a big problem of living in a bedsit for Christopher?
3. What happened to Toby?
4. Why does Siobhan say that Christopher cannot move in with her?
5. How does Christopher use Sandy to feel safe?

EXAM PRACTICE

Using one or more of the 'Key Quotations to Learn', write a paragraph exploring how the ending of the play **represents** change for Christopher.

Narrative Structure

You must be able to: explain the complexities of the **narrative** structure and what purpose they serve.

How is the play organised?

The play is divided into Part One and Part Two. Although the **action** on stage is **continuous**, it jumps between the present and episodes set in the past enacted from the book Christopher is writing.

Part One ends when Christopher has solved both the original mystery of Who Killed Wellington and the secondary mystery of the letters that he uncovered through his detecting.

This moment signals a shift in the narrative; Part Two starts with Christopher facing a new challenge of getting to London.

How does Stephens use Christopher's book as a narrative device?

This is a play about a boy with Asperger's Syndrome who writes a book about his experience of trying to find out Who Killed Wellington.

The Wellington plot forms the basis of the play's storyline but is also used as a way for Stephens to present the key challenges Christopher faces. Siobhan's **narration** of Christopher's book reveals Christopher's thinking processes and his responses to everyday situations.

Why does the action seem to jump about so much?

Some of the story is narrated from Christopher's book, which is interwoven with the drama acted out by Christopher and the other characters.

The events in Part One are not presented in a **chronological** order; they jump between Wellington's story and Christopher's **reflections** in his book so the audience can understand both the plot and Christopher's character at the same time.

Stephens also includes **flashbacks** and memories in Christopher's book to highlight aspects of Christopher's life and his relationships.

At points, the action on stage occurs in different times and locations at the same time. For example, if Siobhan is narrating a part of Christopher's book we know that the action must have already happened, even if we can see Christopher acting it on the stage as though in the present.

Part Two is more straightforward and the plot evolves as one continuous piece of action.

Are there are other narrative twists?

At the start of Part Two, we learn that the school has suggested turning Christopher's book into a play.

We are reminded that we are watching this play within Stephens' play when the action is interrupted by Christopher directing the actors on stage or when he tells Reverend Peters that he is too old to play the part of a policeman.

Key Quotations to Learn

Siobhan: 'This is good, Christopher. It's quite exciting.' (Part One)

Siobhan (speaking from Christopher's story): 'Mother died two years ago.' (Part One)

Siobhan: 'I was wondering if you'd like to make a play out of your book.' (Part Two)

Christopher: 'I'm going to London.' (Part Two)

Summary

- The action of the play is not chronological. The plot about Wellington is interrupted with narration from Christopher's book.
- Stephens uses Christopher's book as a way of highlighting key aspects of his character, relationships and life before Wellington was killed.
- The narrative changes direction when Christopher solves the mysteries but is faced with the new challenge of finding his way to London as a result.
- It turns out that Christopher's book is also turned into a play, creating a play within a play.

Questions

QUICK TEST
1. How does Stephens manage to unfold the plot and highlight Christopher's Asperger's at the same time?
2. Why is the play not chronological?
3. Why does the narrative change direction?
4. When does this take place?
5. What is the play within the play?

EXAM PRACTICE
Using one or more of the 'Key Quotations to Learn', write a paragraph highlighting how Stephens uses the structure of the play to present key features of Christopher's life.

Dramatic Technique

You must be able to: recognise the dramatic techniques used in the play and their effect on the audience.

How does the play use an ensemble cast?

Other than the main characters, Christopher, Ed, Judy and Siobhan, the rest of the cast play multiple parts.

Regardless of whether they are involved in the action at any particular point, they all stay on stage throughout the play *'unless otherwise prescribed'* (Christopher is alone on stage for the first time when he arrives in London and is left hiding on the luggage rack in the train after everyone else has got off).

Practically, the presence of the actors on stage allows for the quick changing of the scenes. Their observation of Christopher from the outskirts of the stage puts him at the centre of the action, **symbolising** his single-minded focus and inability to see the world from another person's point of view.

Theatrically, the actors remind the audience that they are watching the construction of a play, highlighting the making of Christopher's own play.

How are all the various settings of the play presented on stage?

The action of the play takes place in various locations in Swindon and London.

The focus moves quickly between locations, making it impossible to change the **set** for each scene. The audience are required to imagine the location of each scene through the **dialogue** and action on stage.

In some instances, the **company** actors are used to create the noises or physical features of a particular **setting**.

How do we see Christopher's point of view?

Reflective moments that interrupt the action, such as when Christopher is explaining how much he sees in comparison to an ordinary person, explain some of his thinking processes.

Siobhan's narration of Christopher's book is also used to pinpoint key **characteristics** Christopher has highlighted about himself, such as how he 'finds people confusing'.

The company are used to **enact** the conditions in which Christopher becomes uncomfortable, allowing the audience to experience them first hand. For example, the many signs Christopher reads in the train station are spoken aloud creating a 'cacophonous' jumble of noise, which matches the confusion Christopher feels inside his mind. When Christopher is standing on the platform in the tube station, the company 'stand with' him allowing the audience to **visualise** his sense of being uncomfortably crowded in the presence of strangers.

Key Quotations to Learn

Stage directions: *'The company cheer, as if a goal has been scored.'* (Part Two)

Stage directions: *'The company stand with Christopher on the platform.'* (Part Two)

Siobhan: 'Look, why don't you tell it after the curtain call?' (Part Two)

Summary

- The **ensemble** cast play a variety of roles and stay on stage all the time, this puts Christopher at the centre of the action.
- The company create the different settings and noises of the play.
- Sometimes, the company represent the stress Christopher feels in situations.
- The narration of reflective moments in Christopher's book shows us things from his point of view.

Questions

QUICK TEST

1. What is the advantage of having all the actors on stage all the time?
2. When is the first time Christopher is alone on stage?
3. Being surrounded by these actors could be seen as a symbol of what?
4. What is one example of when the company are used to overwhelm Christopher?
5. Why is Siobhan used to narrate Christopher's book rather than anyone else?

EXAM PRACTICE

Using one or more of the 'Key Quotations to Learn', write a paragraph explaining how the writer uses dramatic devices to highlight key features of the play.

Asperger's Syndrome

You must be able to: understand the main features of Asperger syndrome and how these may be evidenced in Christopher's character.

What is Asperger syndrome?

Asperger syndrome is a form of autism. About 700,00 people in the United Kingdom are on the autism spectrum, including those with Asperger syndrome.

Autism is a lifelong developmental disability that affects how people interact with the world around them. You cannot catch autism and, currently, it cannot be cured. Autism is a 'spectrum disorder', which means that there are some people who have a mild form of the disability whilst others further along the spectrum can present more symptoms or suffer with those symptoms to a higher degree.

Symptoms of Asperger syndrome are often first noticed from an age when a child starts interacting in social settings, often with other children.

What are some of the key characteristics of Asperger syndrome?

There are a wide variety of symptoms of Asperger syndrome. An individual with Asperger's may experience some or many of the following possible symptoms:

* Difficulty with social skills and interacting with people.
* Do not understand body language and facial expressions.
* Do not like physical contact.
* Appear to lack empathy for other people and their feelings.
* Can be very **literal** in thinking and **direct** in speech.
* Use a **formal** style of speaking.
* Like routine and dislike change to their normal structures or plans.
* Have a limited range of interests, about which they know a great deal.
* Very sensitive and can be easily overstimulated by loud noises, lights, strong tastes or textures.
* Particularly skilled in specific areas such as maths or music.

What significance does Asperger syndrome have in the play?

Christopher's condition is never mentioned by name in the play. However, he does display key characteristics of someone with Asperger's and by his description of the other children, we know that he does not attend a mainstream school.

Christopher's mother suggests that she found elements of looking after Christopher overwhelming and his father uncharacteristically makes fun of Christopher when he is quite stressed himself, calling him the 'memory man'.

People who do not know Christopher often react as though his behaviour is quite odd to them.

However, it is important to remember that Christopher is a **fictional** character. Rather than presenting a definitive guide to Asperger syndrome, he offers the opportunity for the audience to consider life, and its challenges, from a different **perspective**.

Key Quotations to Learn

Stage directions: '*Ed holds his right hand up and spreads his fingers out in a fan.*'

Ed: '… we're not exactly low maintenance, are we?' (Part One)

Judy: 'Because I often thought I couldn't take it any more.' (Part One)

Stage directions: '*To calm himself he counts the cubes of cardinal numbers.*' (Part Two)

Summary

- Asperger syndrome is a form of autism and a spectrum disorder.
- There are a variety of symptoms that people can exhibit to a greater or lesser degree.
- Christopher presents quite a few symptoms of Asperger syndrome.
- Christopher's parents both express some stress in trying to manage the challenges his Asperger's presents.

Questions

QUICK TEST
1. What is Asperger syndrome?
2. With which symptoms of Asperger's does Christopher present?
3. What are Christopher's particular interests?
4. How do the people close to Christopher sometimes react to his behaviour?

EXAM PRACTICE
Using one or more of the 'Key Quotations to Learn', write a paragraph outlining some of Christopher's symptoms of Asperger's and its impact on his life and those around him.

Christopher's World: Swindon and Beyond

You must be able to: understand the significance of the change of setting in the play.

What is Christopher's day-to-day life like?

The **parameters** of Christopher's daily life are quite narrow, probably due to his discomfort with new situations or environments.

He goes to school and to the shop for sweets. There is not much for him to do on Saturdays unless his father takes him out but even these trips are local – the boating lake or a garden centre.

What are Christopher's experiences of the wider world at the start of the play?

Christopher is seen to have experienced distress in the past while doing something outside of his daily experience; watching his mother diving under the waves on holiday in Cornwall and Christmas shopping with large numbers of people in a department store.

When Christopher thinks of life beyond Swindon, he fantasises about living alone in space.

How does the discovery of Wellington impact upon the current limitations of Christopher's life?

From the moment Christopher discovers the dead dog, the parameters of his world start to widen. He is taken to the police station – a new setting outside of his daily routine – after which he decides to embark on a new project to find out Who Killed Wellington.

Christopher's detecting shows new initiative, approaching unfamiliar neighbours for information. His project causes him to behave secretly at times and defy some of his father's commands but it is through this persistence that Christopher discovers his mother's letters and that she is still alive.

Why is the journey to London significant?

Christopher has never travelled beyond the normal parameters of his daily life on his own.

He is overwhelmed by the noise and huge amount of information available on signs in the train stations. He is uncomfortable speaking to strangers and using shared public facilities.

Christopher's desire to be safe and his need to achieve his objective require him to control his fear. He does well to overcome each new challenge on his journey to London, although there are points where he is evidently stressed; the station policeman found him in a 'complete trance'.

Ironically, he applies features of his Asperger's, such as counting, to calm himself down and creates rhythms and patterns to feel more in control of the unfamiliar environments.

Nevertheless, his limited awareness is made evident when he climbs onto the tracks of the tube.

What is the impact of this journey for Christopher?

Significantly, not everything is resolved once Christopher arrives at his mother's. In discovering the lies his father was hiding, Christopher has uncovered an **ironic** truth – life cannot be defined in black or white terms. He must learn to tolerate a less definite reality.

Christopher has been on both a physical and a metaphoric journey. His travel to London symbolises the process he has undergone to gain some independence and a more mature, informed understanding of the world.

Key Quotations to Learn

Stage directions: *'He makes his hand into a telescope to limit his field of vision.'* (Part Two)

Christopher: 'I can't see any stars here.' (Part Two)

Christopher: 'I don't like waiting for my A-Level result.' (Part Two)

Christopher: 'I can because I went to London on my own.' (Part Two)

Summary

- Christopher lives in a limited world that does not extend beyond his house, street and school.
- The discovery of Wellington starts to change Christopher's life as he is exposed to more people and places.
- He is overwhelmed by the sights, sounds and interactions of travelling.
- He uses practical **strategies** and coping mechanisms to calm himself down and work out his plans.
- Christopher is more mature and has a more confident sense of what he can achieve by the end of the play.

Questions

QUICK TEST
1. What are the limitations of Christopher's daily life at the start of the play?
2. How does the death of Wellington impact on Christopher's character?
3. Why is he overwhelmed at the train station?
4. Why is arriving in London not a perfect resolution?
5. What has Christopher achieved through this journey?

EXAM PRACTICE
Using one or more of the 'Key Quotations to Learn', write a paragraph analysing how the change in setting impacts on Christopher's character.

You must be able to: understand the play in performance.

Where does the play come from?

Stephens' play *The Curious Incident of the Dog in the Night-Time* is based on Mark Haddon's hugely successful novel of the same name.

The original book is written from Christopher's point of view. Through Siobhan suggesting that Christopher converts his own book into a play, Stephens was able to present Christopher's **first person perspective** in his play.

The National Theatre production is the only commercial production of the play. It has won many awards in the UK, including Best New Play, and in the United States, where it has gone on tour.

How do I read the play?

A play is written with the intention that the outcome is performed. When reading a play, you must imagine how it would work on stage.

A play is made up of dialogue that is spoken aloud and action created by actors on stage. The **stage directions** indicate the writer's intention of how the performance should look and feel.

How can Christopher's story be brought to life on stage?

It is important that through performance the audience gets a clear sense of the way Christopher thinks as well as the challenges he faces.

The National Theatre production attempts to present the play as though from inside Christopher's mind, which is shown to be ordered, and represents his interests by lining the floor and walls of the set with mathematical graph paper on which Christopher physically draws his thoughts.

The 'Movement Directors' of the National Theatre production are a theatre company called Frantic Assembly. As Stephens directs that '*all actors remain on stage unless otherwise prescribed*', they **devised** a very physical presentation of the play using all of the members of the ensemble cast to bring Christopher's thoughts to life.

Other than the main characters, the ensemble play multiple roles and can be used to act out Christopher's memories and create sets – as the focus and setting of his book changes so quickly, it is hard to create a fixed set – such as the train stations.

In the National Theatre production, the ensemble also physically interact with Christopher to visually create the reflections from his imagination, carrying him above their heads, for example, when he is describing living in space as an astronaut.

How do the ensemble cast create subtext in production?

Although the ensemble cast are there to support Christopher, they sometimes create **dramatic irony** by communicating with the audience in ways that Christopher does not recognise.

They **foreshadow** his discovery of the affair by creating a tense **tableau** after Ed shouts 'I will not have that man's name mentioned in my house' and '*cheer as if a goal has been scored*' when Christopher makes a positive decision not to get in any more trouble by leaving Mrs Alexander.

Key Quotations to Learn

Stage directions: '*The rest of the company watch, waiting to see who is going to dare to speak first.*' (Part One)

Stage directions: '*Mrs Shears' house is assembled.*' (Part One)

Stage directions: '*Nobody gives Ed a clue as to where Christopher is.*' (Part Two)

Summary

- Stephens' play seeks to maintain the same first person perspective of the original novel from which it is adapted.
- Plays are made up of dialogue and action; the stage directions give guidance on how the writer wants these to be presented.
- Any production of this play needs to visually interpret and present Christopher's thoughts, memories and reflections.
- The National Theatre production of the play is very physical, using the ensemble cast to create the sets and thoughts in Christopher's imagination.
- Christopher is unaware that the ensemble cast also communicate meaning with the audience that he does not understand.

Questions

QUICK TEST
1. Both the book and the play are written from which perspective?
2. What are the key elements of a play?
3. How can Christopher's thoughts be brought to life on stage?
4. How is dramatic irony created in the play?

EXAM PRACTICE

Using one or more of the 'Key Quotations to Learn', write a paragraph analysing how the ensemble cast can be used in performance to highlight key features of Christopher's thinking.

Christopher Boone

You must be able to: analyse how Christopher is presented in the play.

How is Christopher's Asperger's made evident to the audience?

We learn about Christopher's thinking both through his language – the way he talks to people and tells the stories in his book – and actions. He always states himself directly and can explicitly detail some features of his condition, such as 'I don't tell lies'.

The audience must also perceive features of his character through the **subtext** of the responses of other characters to him, such as his parents' separate expressions of the stress he appears to cause.

Dramatic irony is created in situations where the audience understands something in the social world of which Christopher is unaware. He doesn't understand Mrs Alexander when she says 'I think you know why your father doesn't like Mr Shears very much' but the audience can interpret that Judy had an affair.

Christopher's difficulty with emotion, and his preference for facts and logic, can be seen when he asks 'what kind of heart attack?' in response to news that his mother has died. When he finally realises that she is alive he is physically sick, rather than expressing emotional feelings.

How is Christopher's personal development presented in the play?

At the start of the play, Christopher exists in his own world, unable to recognise others' emotions or communicate effectively with them.

When he is making plans for his future at the end, he explicitly recognises his recent growth by stating 'I can do these things'. He is also more aware of his impact on others when he asks Siobhan 'is it because I'm noisy and sometimes I'm "difficult to control?"'

He starts to recognise differences between his thinking and others, asking his mother 'Is killing Wellington a little crime' when he learns that his father will not be prosecuted.

He develops a greater degree of tolerance. Just like his need to find security obliged him to overcome his fears, his desire to feel and express love with his new dog facilitates his disregard of its 'sandy' colour (a mixture of yellow and brown) without recognition of the stress this would have previously created.

What purpose does Christopher serve in the play?

Christopher's quest to find security compels his parents to take responsibility for their own actions and reprioritise his needs, both as a child as well as someone with a developmental disability.

Through Christopher, Stephens presents an experience of being 'different' that challenges the audience to consider what is 'normal'. All of us have the capacity to say or do seemingly strange things, such as Ed maintaining the fabrication that Judy was dead. Christopher's struggle and success in dealing with the challenges of his condition dares the audience to ask more of themselves.

Key Quotations to Learn

Christopher: 'I know all the countries of the world ...' (Part One)

Ed: 'She has a problem ... a problem with her heart.' (Part One)

Siobhan (speaking from Christopher's story): 'Mother died two years ago.' (Part One)

Summary

- Christopher is **explicit** about some features of his Asperger's.
- Dramatic irony is created when the audience interpret things of which Christopher is unaware through his language and actions.
- Subtext is created through other characters' responses to Christopher.
- Christopher's achievements challenge his parents and the audience to be better themselves.

Sample Analysis

Christopher's change can be seen as a typical stage of growing up, as well as an important challenge to the limitations of his Asperger's. When he says 'I will be a scientist' he is making an independent statement of intention, just like any other teenager deciding what to do with their life. However, for Christopher, this is even more profound as it shows not only that he now recognises his potential but wants to apply it to achieve a more 'normal' life, which he would not have previously considered.

Questions

QUICK TEST
1. Name one feature of his condition of which Christopher is aware.
2. When is there dramatic irony?
3. How does Christopher change in the play?
4. What does Christopher represent in this play?

EXAM PRACTICE
Using one or more of the 'Key Quotations to Learn', write a paragraph analysing the presentation of Christopher in the play.

Ed Boone

You must be able to: analyse how Ed is presented in the play.

What are the challenges facing Ed?

He is a single parent and Christopher has very specific needs that create more work for him.

Ed has been rejected by both his wife and then Mrs Shears. He is carrying his self-made secrets of Judy's departure and Wellington's death.

Ed may be lonely. He is unhappily single and his relationship with Christopher is quite practical. In addition to Christopher's own struggles with communication, in one of her letters, Judy says that Ed 'just gets on with things and if things upset him he doesn't let it show'.

How is it made clear to the audience that Ed is experiencing some stress?

Ed's language changes when he is stressed:

- He shouts and swears.
- He becomes sarcastic (both at school and when he is arguing with Christopher).
- He rants, saying significantly more than usual.
- He makes his point by overwhelming Christopher with lots of questions that he can't process quickly.

There is a sense that Ed is somewhat hot-headed – he talks of the 'red mist' coming down when he killed Wellington and during his fight with Christopher he '*throws Christopher's book*' and '*grabs Christopher's arm*'.

What is the audience led to feel about Ed?

Although he does not always understand him, Ed clearly loves his son. He is familiar with Christopher's specific needs and takes good physical care of him. He is playful with Christopher, calling him 'mate' and asking what he wants for 'chow'.

It is evident that Ed can be a 'patient person'. When he picks Christopher up from the police station, the first thing he does is hold out his hand to show that he loves him. He fights for Christopher's chance to take his A-Level Maths, recognising its value for Christopher.

However, in the eyes of the audience he has made some major mistakes: first, his physical fight with Christopher; second, he lied about Judy's death to Christopher and concealed her letters.

Ed may have been feeling pressure at the time, and we do sense he feels genuine remorse, but these actions are not easily forgivable. His attempts to explain himself to Christopher suggest a need to be heard or feel some support himself but Christopher is both too young and has too limited an emotional range to understand these pleas.

By the end of the play, Ed has taken full responsibility for his actions. He accepts the need to rebuild their relationship at Christopher's **pace** and in a style he can respond well to.

Key Quotations to Learn

Stage directions: *'Ed stares at him. Says nothing.'* (Part One)

Ed: 'It's a bloody dog, Christopher, a bloody dog.' (Part One)

Ed: 'Christopher, can I have a talk with you?' (Part Two)

Summary

- There are a variety of challenges facing Ed.
- Ed and Christopher are not similar characters but they clearly share a strong loving bond.
- Ed looks after Christopher's physical needs well.
- Ed is described as 'patient' but he acts impulsively when he is stressed.
- He has made some significant mistakes, which he must take responsibility for and seek to resolve.

Sample Analysis

A significant part of Ed's stress is caused by the secrets he is keeping. When he shouts 'I will not have that man's name mentioned in my house', the possessive description of his property **implicitly** suggests that Ed feels threatened and needs to protect what is close to him. However, when the company 'pause to look at Ed and Christopher' we understand that Christopher does not know why his father is agitated. Ironically, Ed's attempts to control the situation result in his worst fears as he loses Christopher when he uncovers the truth.

Questions

QUICK TEST

1. Name two challenges that Ed has to deal with.
2. List two ways in which we can see that Ed is stressed.
3. What shows that Ed loves Christopher?
4. What is Ed's responsibility at the end of the play?

EXAM PRACTICE

Using one or more of the 'Key Quotations to Learn', write a paragraph analysing the presentation of Ed in the play.

Judy Boone

You must be able to: analyse how Judy is presented in the play.

What do Christopher's memories tell us about his mother?

Christopher remembers his mother diving under the waves at the beach while on holiday in Cornwall. The memory gives us the impression that Judy was quite carefree. However, when Christopher became upset she immediately reassured him and showed she loved him by putting up her hand in a fan.

Christopher has another memory of his mother playfully talking about the life she would have led if she had not married Ed. The image she paints of living in the countryside in France contrasts starkly with her reality in Swindon, hinting at her unhappiness and foreshadowing her eventual departure.

What do her letters to Christopher reveal about Judy?

Rather than argue about the stress they felt and their different attitudes towards looking after Christopher, Judy and Ed stopped talking altogether. This was how an emotional distance formed that Judy solved by speaking to Mr Shears.

Judy says she didn't want to leave Christopher but felt that he didn't need her as he appeared to be so much calmer when Ed was looking after him. She was heartbroken about this but thought it would be 'better for us all' if she left.

However, through the letters, Judy has tried to maintain her relationship with Christopher. Unlike Ed, Judy is trying to be honest with Christopher, showing respect for his right to an explanation.

What is the audience's experience of Judy when we finally meet her?

Judy may be lonely in London. She is arguing with Roger when we first meet them and tries to hug Christopher when he arrives, forgetting that he does not like physical contact.

Judy may be desperate for some contact with her son but it could be interpreted that she sometimes struggles to put Christopher's needs before her own. She is dismissive of his maths exam and postpones it rather than organise the logistics of getting him there.

She also still finds Christopher's behaviour stressful. Statements such as 'I swear to God, Christopher, I love you, but …' sound conditional and create tension for the audience who do not want to see Christopher lose either parent again.

However, she seems determined to make a better go at this second chance. It is clear that Roger is not happy to accept Christopher and she leaves Roger as soon as he becomes threatening.

Despite being angry with Ed, she recognises his value in Christopher's life and works with him to create a new routine through which Ed and Christopher can rebuild their relationship.

Key Quotations to Learn

Judy: '… I wanted to explain to you why I went away …' (Part One)

Judy: 'I used to have dreams that everything would get better.' (Part One)

Stage directions: '*Judy starts to howl*.' (Part Two)

Summary

- We learn things about Judy through Christopher's memories and through her letters before we meet her.
- She seems to be a playful and loving character who felt trapped and stressed in her life at home.
- At times, Judy struggles with the conflict of her own needs against Christopher's.
- She is protective of Christopher after they meet again and works hard to build a new life for them.

Sample Analysis

Judy feels that she 'was not a very good mother' when she was living at home. She appears to make this judgement of herself in comparison to Ed who could more easily shrug off stress associated with Christopher by saying 'these things happen'. Ironically, the audience can easily understand that she felt challenged by the circumstances of her life and would not have judged her harshly in the first instance. They might even have forgiven her affair but the move to London is so drastic we might be inclined to agree that it was not a 'good' decision for a 'mother' to make.

Questions

QUICK TEST
1. What were Judy's dreams?
2. Why did she leave home?
3. How do we know Judy loves Christopher?
4. What struggles must she overcome to be with Christopher?

EXAM PRACTICE
Using one or more of the 'Key Quotations to Learn', write a paragraph analysing the presentation of Judy in the play.

Christopher's Teacher: Siobhan

You must be able to: analyse how Siobhan is presented in the play.

What is Siobhan's relationship with Christopher?

As Christopher's teacher, Siobhan acts as mentor and friend to Christopher throughout the play. She teaches him how to understand other people and she is the only character who asks Christopher genuine questions about his emotions.

She is gently honest with Christopher, helping him find solutions but without putting pressure on him. She ensures he is in control of his own decisions, for example, checking that he really does want to take his maths exam.

We do not find out any personal information about Siobhan; their relationship is led by Christopher's needs. With her, Christopher is able to share his ideas and confide his concerns.

How does Siobhan help Christopher with his book?

Siobhan is the only character in the play who really seems to understand how Christopher thinks.

She suggests he writes about Wellington and she helps him turn his book into a play.

Stephens symbolises the intellectual connection they share by interchanging Christopher's descriptions of events with Siobhan's narration of sections from Christopher's book on stage.

How is stagecraft used to highlight Siobhan's support of Christopher?

In Part Two, the audience feel as though they are watching Christopher's live thought processes as he negotiates his way across London.

Even though Siobhan is not present in reality, her impact on his thoughts and decisions at the time are highlighted by her presence on stage and live interactions with Christopher.

When Christopher is stressed at the train station, Siobhan appears in his mind and on stage advising him to visualise a big red line across the floor and 'count the rhythm in your head'.

She is present when he is scared of sleeping in London, chatting to him as though in his mind, and she appears again during his maths exam, calming him down by focussing his attention on maths patterns.

What are the limitations of Siobhan's relationship with Christopher?

Siobhan is clearly fond of Christopher. She displays emotional pride in his achievement, stuttering 'Oh. Oh. That's just. That's just terrific Christopher' when he reads his A* A-Level Maths result.

However, as his teacher, she must remain neutral and defer to the authority of his parents. She expresses regret but supports Ed's decision that the book cannot be continued. Later, when Christopher asks why he can't live with her she says 'I'm not your mother Christopher'.

Each of these situations is hard for Christopher to accept but the clear boundaries that Siobhan sets play an important role in teaching Christopher about appropriate behaviour in relationships.

Key Quotations to Learn

Siobhan (speaking from Christopher's story): 'Siobhan says that if you raise one eyebrow it can mean lots of different things.' (Part One)

Siobhan: 'Did it make you sad to find this out?' (Part One)

Siobhan: 'We turned it into a play.' (Part Two)

Summary

- Siobhan understands Christopher's mind better than the other characters do.
- Siobhan cares for Christopher's emotional wellbeing as well as his intellectual pursuits.
- She guides Christopher in understanding the world and taking appropriate action in it.
- Christopher's connection to Siobhan is represented through her 'appearances' in his mind on stage.
- Siobhan maintains professional boundaries with Christopher.

Sample Analysis

Siobhan plays a significant role in Christopher's development towards greater independence. It is appropriate that she is with him when he opens his A-Level result and she is the last person he talks to in the play. His final statement is a repetition of his own question 'Does that mean I can do anything, Siobhan?' but without the inclusion of her name. This suggests he is ultimately asking himself the question and symbolises his final leap of independence from the security she offered to a belief that he can face his own challenges.

Questions

QUICK TEST

1. Why don't we learn about Siobhan's personal life?
2. How is Siobhan's presence on stage used to highlight their relationship?
3. How does Siobhan help Christopher when he leaves Swindon?
4. Why can't Christopher live with Siobhan?

EXAM PRACTICE

Using one or more of the 'Key Quotations to Learn', write a paragraph analysing the presentation of Siobhan in the play.

Mrs Alexander, Mrs Shears and Mr Shears (Roger)

You must be able to: analyse the roles the supporting characters have in the play.

How does Mrs Alexander help move on the action of the play?

Christopher meets Mrs Alexander when he is detecting in his street. She is an elderly lady who has a grandson about Christopher's age; this allows a connection to be made.

Mrs Alexander is aware of Christopher and is friendly towards him. She makes efforts to accommodate his idiosyncrasies – refusal to come inside or eat Battenberg cake – without making fun of him or seeming frustrated by his needs.

It is Mrs Alexander who reveals that Christopher's mother had an affair with Mr Shears – this leads to the discovery of the letters and the change in direction of the narrative.

How does Mrs Shears represent the wider world of Christopher's neighbourhood?

It seems likely that Christopher only met Mrs Shears because his mother left. Otherwise, as with most other people on his street, his relative lack of knowledge about her symbolises the limited boundaries of his experience at the start of the play.

Mrs Shears is the first character to speak in the play. She establishes a heightened sense of drama in the opening scene through shouting and swearing at Christopher.

She is obviously very upset but the audience is likely to feel surprised by the aggressive language she uses with a young person.

Her manner is repeated by various people throughout the play, highlighting the additional challenge Christopher has in managing the responses of those who are bemused by his character.

How is Roger presented in comparison to Ed?

We first meet Roger when he is in the middle of an argument with Judy, indicating that all is not well between them.

The arguments Judy had with Ed were focussed on her struggle to care for Christopher and the stress it caused. Without these problems to consider in London her problems with Roger seem to be about how they relate to one another.

There is a nasty undertone to the final scene when Roger is drunk and 'grabs at Christopher'. There is a sense that he intends to harm Christopher, who seems intimidated and 'rolls himself into a ball to hide'.

This contrasts with the sudden spontaneity of Ed and Christopher's wrangle in which Christopher fights back.

Key Quotations to Learn

Mrs Shears: 'Get away from my dog.' (Part One)

Mrs Alexander: 'I'm not a stranger, Christopher, I'm a friend.' (Part One)

Roger: 'You think you're so clever, don't you?' (Part Two)

Summary

- Mrs Alexander tells Christopher about his mother's affair with Mr Shears. She considers herself a friend to Christopher.

- Mrs Shears is representative of Christopher's vague connections to his neighbours and therefore his limited experience of life outside his own home.

- Mr Shears is visibly frustrated by Christopher and is nasty to him. Mr Shears' failings highlight Ed's qualities, however flawed.

Sample Analysis

Roger is a weak character who could never offer a credible alternative to Ed. Whilst we cannot expect him to care for Christopher as his father would, Roger is instinctively dismissive of Christopher, as well as as of Judy's attempts to look after him. One of his first comments on Christopher's arrival is 'I suppose this means Ed's here?' displaying a selfish lack of concern for both Judy and Christopher. Even when he appears to make an effort by buying Christopher books, his disinterest in understanding Christopher's character is evident through the inappropriate selection he makes. Roger's sarcastic response to Christopher's rejection of them once again focusses attention back on himself by suggesting the only reason for buying the books is so that he could be 'appreciated'.

Questions

QUICK TEST

1. What does Mrs Alexander share in common with Christopher?
2. What does Mrs Alexander tell him about his mother?
3. What is inappropriate about the way Mrs Shears speaks to Christopher?
4. What is the audience's view of Mr Shears?

EXAM PRACTICE

Using one or more of the 'Key Quotations to Learn', write a paragraph analysing what Christopher's interactions with the supporting characters show us about his connections to the wider world.

You must be able to: analyse how the characters change over the course of the play.

Do the characters change?

The three characters of the Boone family – Christopher, Ed and Judy – change over the course of the play. The other main character, Siobhan, does not undergo a significant change. She exists as a steady influence in Christopher's life, offering balance and reason to his messy family circumstances.

Christopher

At the start of the play, Christopher lives a sheltered life showing little interest beyond his daily routine.

The discovery of Wellington intrudes on this normality and sets Christopher on a new path. He makes his first independent decision to find out Who Killed Wellington and then pursues his investigation despite his father's instructions otherwise.

The journey to London is a turning point for Christopher. Although he is disturbed by exposure to people and new environments, he uses a variety of strategies to manage his responses so that he can find his mother.

Against significant odds, Christopher achieves what he set out to – both in solving Who Killed Wellington and in getting to London. He develops in confidence through this experience and by the end of the play expresses new ambitions for an independent future.

Ed

It is not clear when Ed would have told Christopher the truth about his mother, although, when it does happen, he acknowledges that it is better out in the open. Christopher has unwittingly done Ed a favour as maintaining the lie was an unknown barrier in their relationship, which they can both now move on from.

Ed has had a difficult two years and his actions might be understood as a result of the pressures he feels. However, he must take responsibility for the consequences of his poor decisions. By the end of the play, he accepts that although he struggles to express it, Christopher also has an emotional life that must be respected as equal to his own.

Judy

Even while she was living in Swindon, Judy wanted to change. She struggled to cope with the day-to-day practicalities of looking after Christopher and dreamed of a life away from her husband.

In moving to London with Roger, Judy achieves respite from each of these situations but does not solve her problems. She does not appear particularly happy with Roger and misses Christopher.

Christopher's appearance offers Judy a second chance at motherhood. She is still challenged by the demands of caring for him and is angry with Ed but she understands the importance of their relationship and takes action to ensure Christopher's needs are met.

Key Quotations to Learn

Christopher: 'I solved the mystery of Who Killed Wellington.' (Part Two)

Ed: '… if you don't tell the truth now, then later on it hurts even more.' (Part One)

Judy: 'We're going to the school.' (Part Two)

Summary

- The discovery of Wellington triggers changes – starting with Christopher's investigations.
- Christopher imposes change on his parents through his determination to achieve his own aims.
- Ed understands that Christopher has emotional needs that must be valued.
- Judy learns to accommodate Christopher's needs alongside her own.

Sample Analysis

Although Christopher starts to change first in the play, in killing Wellington, Ed can be seen as the catalyst for this change. When Christopher asks Ed whether he is sad about Wellington's death he responds, 'Yes Christopher you could say that', the **modal verb** 'could' suggesting some hesitancy, although he has replied positively. We later understand that Ed was sad about the circumstances that led up to Wellington's death and all the secrets he has maintained since. However, it seems as though he is unable to honestly explain himself and is dropping hints to the audience that there is more to the story than he has revealed.

Questions

QUICK TEST

1. In what way is Christopher's life sheltered at the start of the play?
2. What triggers change in the play?
3. How does Christopher force Ed to change?
4. What change can we see in Judy?

EXAM PRACTICE

Using one or more of the 'Key Quotations to Learn', write a paragraph analysing how the changes in each of the main characters benefit all of the Boone family.

Difference

You must be able to: analyse the meaning and presentation of difference in the play.

What does 'difference' mean?

'Difference' suggests something other than a perceived idea of a 'normal' standard. Through Christopher, Stephens presents a version of being 'different' in contrast to other people who, not being on the autism spectrum, would commonly be perceived as 'normal'.

Does different mean less good?

The stress caused by Christopher's Asperger's is not positive. Conversely, he has an advanced understanding of maths which may be very beneficial to him in the future.

Ironically, the struggle to celebrate difference is **symbolised** through Mrs Gascoyne. As headmistress of a school for children with special needs, she sees herself as someone who manages the difficulties of difference rather than finding the potential within the children. To her, 'everyone' wanting to be 'treated differently', if she allowed Christopher to sit his Maths A-Level, is a bad thing.

How is difference judged in this play?

Stephens suggests that people are often challenged by difference and use it as an opportunity for derision or abuse.

Roger attacks Christopher for being different but also seems threatened by it. He separates Christopher from himself on the basis of his significant intelligence but then blames him for having it, suggesting Christopher applies it with malign intent towards others.

The drunken passenger who discovers Christopher hiding on the luggage rack calls his friend over to look as though he is an object of curiosity, depersonalising him as a 'train elf'. They assume a superiority to Christopher and feel empowered to ridicule him as though his difference is not deserving of normal standards of social interaction.

Even Christopher judges the children in his school for being 'stupid', which he sees as different to himself.

What is the purpose of difference in the play?

Stephens warns against viewing a singular point of difference as a defining characteristic. There are points in the play where seemingly 'normal' people behave oddly or poorly whilst Christopher can be seen as quite honourable at times. Neither of his parents are seen as 'different', but they each let him down in some way, whereas Christopher makes a commitment to 'never do anything to hurt' his new dog.

Characters who are accepting or engaged with Christopher's difference – such as Siobhan and Mrs Alexander – symbolise the possibility that being different in society is either not so strange or not a barrier against reasonable relations with other people.

Key Quotations to Learn

Christopher: 'I think some dogs are cleverer than some people.' (Part One)

Mrs Alexander: 'Yes I think you could probably describe it like that.' (Part One)

Drunk One: 'Come and look at this, Barry.' (Part Two)

Summary

- Christopher is presented as the main person of 'difference' in this play.
- His difference causes both him and his family stress but brings some advantages as well.
- Many people don't like difference or they don't understand it.
- Everyone can seem different sometimes. Even seemingly 'normal' characters do odd things.
- Mrs Alexander shows that when difference is accepted it seems less problematic and strange.

Sample Analysis

A key message of the play is that difference is not always negative. Although Christopher struggles to communicate, he is also capable of doing remarkable things that most other 'normal' people will never manage. Rhodri has already had to admit that he doesn't 'have a bloody clue' how to answer the maths question he has asked Christopher when he tries to make fun of his 'little bottle of red paint'. The **adjective** 'little' is patronising but instead Christopher makes him look foolish by saying that paint would be 'extremely dangerous' to which even Ed calls him a 'Plonker!'

Questions

QUICK TEST

1. Why does Christopher's difference cause stress?
2. What is Mrs Gascoyne's concern about fully accommodating Christopher's needs?
3. How do people commonly respond to difference in others?
4. Give one example where an apparently normal character does something strange.

EXAM PRACTICE

Using one or more of the 'Key Quotations to Learn', write a paragraph analysing Stephens' purpose in presenting difference in the play.

Loss

You must be able to: explore how loss is presented in the play.

What is lost in the play?

1. The first two 'deaths' in the play are dramatic and impact upon the plot. The action of the play begins with the discovery of Wellington and moves in a new direction again when Christopher discovers that his mother is in fact not dead. Toby's death is more natural, according to the lifespan of a rat – it is symbolic that this happens when Christopher's life has regained its sense of stability.

2. Loss in relationships is seen through the separation of Judy and Ed and the failure of each of them to gain long-term security in romance afterwards. Judy unwittingly loses her relationship with Christopher through leaving, whereas Ed loses his relationship with Christopher through the lies he has told. Love is presented as both precious and precarious and not to be taken for granted, even in a family.

3. Some loss of identity is evident, particularly for Judy who initially seemed to struggle with the responsibilities in her life preventing her from being the kind of person she dreamed of. Ed's lies may have been an attempt to protect Christopher but in assuming that he cannot manage the complex reasons for his mother's departure, Ed has denied him any emotional connection as well as the truth.

4. Through his discoveries and subsequent journey to London, Christopher loses an innocence that his Asperger's may have helped to maintain longer than would be natural for many children. He learns many things about the world and himself which, had he not been compelled to, he may have taken far longer to learn.

How do the characters deal with loss?

Christopher does not feel emotion in the same way as other people. He is blunt about the discovery of Wellington but feels a practical need to resolve the murder. His first response on hearing that his mother has died is to enquire how, rather than to express regret.

Ed's lie about Judy's death makes it difficult for him to talk about her at all. He maintains a functional relationship with Christopher but on false pretences – it could be said that the integrity of their relationship was lost even before Christopher left home.

Judy, in comparison, does appear to attempt some honesty with Christopher but this is done from some distance through her letters. We cannot say when Christopher would have been reunited with Judy had he not found her and it is clear that she accepts she must do more on a day-to-day basis to consider his needs.

Summary

- There is a variety of both physical and emotional loss in the play.
- Some loss in life is inevitable but there is dramatic and unexpected loss in the play, which is used to drive the plot.
- Christopher manages the death of others through practical reasoning rather than as an emotional expression.
- Judy wants to talk about loss; Ed bottles it up.

Sample Analysis

Although Christopher does not express particular distress at the loss of his mother, her 'death' still seems to have been of some significance to him. We first sense he may have been thinking about where his mother has gone when he asks Reverend Peters where heaven is. When he discovers that she is still alive he is sick and then 'lies still for a while, wrapped in a ball'. This extreme physical reaction could be seen as an expression of emotional pain that he has been unable to understand or explain.

Questions

QUICK TEST
1. How many deaths are there in the play?
2. How does Ed get away with his lie about Judy dying?
3. Why does the audience feel some loss for Christopher on discovering that Judy is still alive?
4. What positive loss is the final outcome of the play?

EXAM PRACTICE
Using one or more of the 'Key Quotations to Learn', write a paragraph analysing the effect of loss on the characters in the play.

Communication

You must be able to: analyse how Stephens presents the theme of communication in the play.

Why does communication matter?

Misunderstanding arises through the characters' inability to communicate effectively with one another.

Judy's inability to peacefully discuss with Ed the pressures she feels looking after Christopher leads to her finding comfort with Mr Shears. Ed's inability to effectively communicate with Mrs Shears leads directly to Wellington's death just as Christopher's departure from home is the consequence of Ed's attempts to cover up the truth about that murder as well as Judy and her letters. Christopher's inability to understand social cues of conversation leads to him being arrested for hitting a policeman.

What are the challenges to effective communication in the play?

Christopher has a less developed ability to communicate effectively with people.

He is explicitly aware of some of the issues he experiences, such as trying to make literal sense of metaphoric language.

However, the audience is also aware that Christopher's manner of communication can be exasperating for others and that he is not conscious of the impact he is having. For example, Ed listens to Christopher's descriptive **monologue** on space for a while but he is finally overwhelmed with the one-way flow of information.

Judy's absence from the family home places a physical barrier between her effective communication with her son (via her letters) that Ed is easily able to intercept.

On the other hand, there is an emotional barrier to Ed admitting the truth about the breakdown in his marriage and loss of control with Wellington. When he is finally forced to give his side of the story, he struggles to find words to explain his obvious pain.

Where is good communication demonstrated?

Siobhan is both a teacher and role model of effective communication for Christopher. She helps him find ways to understand others more easily and is persistently honest and understanding of him during their dialogue.

Mrs Alexander speaks to Christopher as an equal. She does not patronise him and trusts him with the truth when it is required for clarity.

By the end of the play, the characters are communicating better. Ed and Judy are able to discuss arrangements and Ed uses the alarm clock to manage his conversations with Christopher to avoid them becoming overwhelmed.

Their new communication may be the most genuine they have ever had, symbolising a new understanding that all young people must negotiate with their parents as they mature into adulthood.

Ironically, Christopher's book very effectively presents his story as he has the narrative freedom to express his thoughts as they occur to him rather than feeling restricted by having to interpret and respond to others. The audience can also be sure that as he 'does not tell lies', this version of events is a true representation of Christopher's point of view.

Key Quotations to Learn

Christopher: '... people do a lot of talking without using any words.' (Part One)

Ed: 'Could you please, just, give it a bit of a break, mate.' (Part One)

Mrs Alexander: '... if I don't explain, you'll carry on wondering what I meant.' (Part One)

Summary

- Christopher's difficulty with communication is linked to his developmental disorder.
- His parents' struggle to **articulate** effectively is due to the physical or emotional restraints their life decisions have imposed upon them.
- Siobhan teaches Christopher how to communicate more effectively and shows him by example.
- Christopher's book effectively communicates exactly what and how he thinks.

Sample Analysis

Although Christopher struggles to communicate, he has developed a range of non-verbal ways of making himself understood. He expresses love with his parents by touching fingers, he makes clear his distress when his mother cancels his exam without speaking to him about it by stopping eating and drinking, and when people get too close to him on his journey to London he '*barks at them like a dog*' to scare them off. The animalistic comparison further emphasises his relative discomfort in engaging with other humans.

Questions

QUICK TEST
1. Why does Christopher find people confusing?
2. Why is not being able to lie not always a good thing?
3. Which character is a consistently good communicator?
4. What makes Mrs Alexander's communication with Christopher good?

EXAM PRACTICE
Using one or more of the 'Key Quotations to Learn', write a paragraph analysing the impact of poor communication in the play.

Relationships

You must be able to: analyse the significance of relationships in the play.

Why are relationships important in the play?

The play shows us that relationships are central to our sense of security and identity. The development and maintenance of relationships requires effort and shared experience and their breakdown can cause significant destabilisation.

The main action of the play is driven by the breakdown of relationships. Wellington's death is caused by the failure of Ed's marriage and his unsuccessful attempt to have a relationship with Mrs Shears. Christopher's journey to London is triggered by the breakdown of his relationship with his dad.

How are relationships used to highlight Christopher's character?

We see different aspects of Christopher's character through his interactions with other people.

His relationship with his dad is very practical. Ed takes care of his physical needs, organising food and making sure he is safe at home.

Ed convinces himself that Christopher is fully cared for but his investigations into Wellington's death symbolise Christopher reaching beyond the organised structure of their shared life. At the end of the play, Ed is required to renegotiate his relationship with Christopher with a new emotional openness that has no space for secrets.

In contrast to the turbulence his relationships with his parents create, Christopher's relationship with Siobhan is seen as a stable influence. She understands the way his mind works and through her narration of his book we see that he trusts her with his most personal thoughts.

Christopher's communication with 'strangers' highlights how difficult it is for him to interact in the wider world. He finds people confusing and strangers are often rude to him as they do not understand his behaviour.

Mrs Alexander is less judgemental, possibly because she is not pressured by time and doesn't get frustrated by trying to accommodate Christopher's needs.

What is Christopher's attitude to relationships?

Christopher takes time to feel comfortable with people and formally classifies his relationships into 'family', 'friend' or 'stranger'. He classifies Mrs Alexander as a 'stranger' due to their short acquaintance, although she sees herself as his 'friend'.

He finds people confusing and is easily overwhelmed when trying to communicate with them. As a result, he enjoys being alone and fantasises about being thousands of miles away from people as an astronaut in space.

However, the desire to find his mother after the breakdown in the relationship with his father shows that Christopher both wants and needs relationships.

Key Quotations to Learn

Christopher: 'Not a friend or member of my family.' (Part One)

Siobhan (speaking from Christopher's story): 'And know that there was no one else near me for thousands and thousands of miles ...' (Part One)

Ed: 'I have to show you that you can trust me.' (Part Two)

Summary

- Breakdowns in relationships lead to the death of Wellington and Christopher leaving home.
- Christopher's communication with strangers shows his difficulties in relating to the wider world.
- Siobhan offers stability and balance for Christopher.
- Although Christopher likes being alone, we can see that he still wants and needs relationships.

Sample Analysis

Although he often fantasises about living alone in space, the audience are made aware that relationships are central to Christopher's life through his constant interaction with the ensemble cast on stage. Christopher knowingly uses Siobhan to narrate parts of the play but, in performance, a whole company helps him act out his thoughts and memories and construct his plans as he journeys to London. As the play presents the story from Christopher's perspective, their presence **signifies** that his view of the world is seen in relation to others. Symbolically, he is only '*alone on stage*' when he arrives in London, marking the definite separation from his old life to a more independent self.

Questions

QUICK TEST

1. What categories does Christopher put his relationships into?
2. How do breakdowns in relationships force things to happen in the play?
3. What are the limitations of Christopher's relationship with his dad?
4. How does Christopher fantasise about escaping relationships?

EXAM PRACTICE

Using one or more of the 'Key Quotations to Learn', write a paragraph analysing what we learn about Christopher's attitude to relationships.

Journey to Independence

You must be able to: track Christopher's journey towards independence across the play.

Why does there need to be a move towards independence?

Christopher's condition means that he is more reliant on the people close to him for practical support than other teenagers generally are at his age.

His daily lifestyle and routines are organised in such a way that he is not particularly exposed to the things he does not like.

Regardless, becoming more independent is a necessary part of growing up.

Conditions compel Christopher to participate in this process sooner than he expected to. This is scary for him, but he is successful in achieving greater confidence and awareness by the end of the play.

What form does the journey take?

Christopher's 'journey' is both physical and personal.

The discovery of Wellington disrupts Christopher's normality and he unknowingly starts on the metaphoric path of personal growth, part of which includes his physical journey from Swindon to his mother's house in London.

Along the way, Christopher has to deal with the struggles in his own mind – his susceptibility to being overwhelmed by places, noises and people – as well as other people's struggle to respond to him appropriately.

He must master his instinct to resort to old behaviours of groaning and screaming to stay practically focussed on achieving his objective.

What happens on the journey?

From the start of the investigation into Who Killed Wellington, Christopher makes all his own decisions:

* he defies his father's instructions to conclude the investigation without knowing who killed Wellington;
* as a result of his persistence he discovers his mother's letters;
* this leads to his father's confession on the basis of which he decides to leave home;
* his determination to find his mother compels him to manage his fear and overcome a series of challenges he has never faced alone before;
* his insistence on sitting his maths exam takes him back to Swindon with his mother; and
* the relationship with his father is formed on a more solid foundation of honesty.

Christopher's exposure to new places and people, and the experience of managing his emotions and creating a plan, makes him feel that there are new and exciting possibilities for his future.

Key Quotations to Learn

Christopher: 'I'm going to find out who killed Wellington.' (Part One)

Christopher: 'I'm going to London.' (Part Two)

Stage directions: *'He starts listing prime numbers to himself.'* (Part Two)

Christopher: 'Then I will be a scientist.' (Part Two)

Summary

- Christopher is compelled by circumstances to begin his journey to independence.
- He makes his own decisions to take action.
- He has to overcome his own fear and others' fear for him.
- He must manage his Asperger's to achieve his objective.
- The process of doing so generates confidence that he can achieve much more in his life.

Sample Analysis

Although Christopher does develop a great deal, there is still a question at the end of the play as to what this really means for his future. Some doubt is suggested in him having to ask 'Does that mean I can do anything?' and while the absence of an answer may symbolise that it is for Christopher to determine now that he has a more clear sense of his capabilities, it may also indicate that Siobhan cannot respond positively or does not know. Perhaps it is naive of the audience to feel that because Christopher's achievements are so remarkable they mean he can do 'anything' at all but then again the same could be said of anyone. Certainly, by the end of the play, Christopher has more experience, confidence and resilience to support him in his attempts to do what he wants.

Questions

QUICK TEST
1. What is the 'journey to independence'?
2. What starts the process of Christopher becoming more independent?
3. Why is the process difficult?
4. In what ways has Christopher developed by the end of the play?

EXAM PRACTICE
Using one or more of the 'Key Quotations to Learn', write a paragraph analysing how we can observe Christopher's development through his language.

Science, Logic and Puzzles

You must be able to: understand the symbolism of science, logic and puzzles in the play.

What does science mean to Christopher?

Christopher's attention to facts and informative detail makes science a suitable interest for him and he is able to absorb and retain large amounts of material.

Symbolically, science highlights the separation between Christopher and other people. He fantasises about being an astronaut living on his own in a confined space operating machines for company. This 'Dream Come True' offers opportunities for Christopher to apply his specific kind of intelligence without being challenged by the things, and people, he does not understand.

Why does logic appeal to Christopher?

Christopher finds metaphors confusing because they require **interpretation**. His mind makes a picture in his head to understand whatever another person is talking about but this doesn't work for metaphors.

On the other hand, just as science is evidence-based, logic requires valid grounds for its reasoning. Christopher can work with this on the basis of what he knows to be true.

Christopher's inability to lie is symbolic of his logical mind.

How does Christopher use puzzles?

Just like his interest in maths, puzzles offer Christopher something to work out using appropriate frameworks, rules and principles.

Christopher uses his interest in patterns and puzzles to his advantage on his journey to London. He finds the train station by 'moving in a spiral' and takes control of his fear in the tube by working out the rhythm of the arriving and departing trains.

Christopher's quest to find out Who Killed Wellington is a type of puzzle to which he can apply his knowledge and logic, for example, working out ordered reasons for why someone would kill a dog. He enjoys the deduction of his detecting process, applying himself as though in a 'real murder mystery novel'.

However, he solves the crime of Who Killed Wellington by accident, highlighting that for all his attempts to create and apply order in his life, the real world does not have such neat solutions.

Key Quotations to Learn

Siobhan (speaking from Christopher's story): 'And know that there was no one else near me for thousands and thousands of miles ...' (Part One)

Siobhan (speaking from Christopher's story): '... imagining an apple in someone's eye doesn't have anything to do with liking someone a lot ...' (Part One)

Christopher: 'Wellington was therefore most likely to have been killed by someone known to him.' (Part One)

Summary

- Science is based on evidence, appealing to Christopher's interest in facts and information.
- Christopher imagines a life in space possibly to avoid the reality of the world.
- Christopher does not like language or images that are not logical.
- Finding out Who Killed Wellington is a kind of puzzle.
- Christopher uses some puzzles to help him on his journey to London, but not all of life is so neat.

Sample Analysis

Science and puzzles symbolise the logical, practical reasoning of Christopher's mind. His reality is rooted in validated facts and information and he struggles to comprehend things that he does not know to be true or which cannot be evidenced. When he asks Reverend Peters to locate heaven he wants to know 'In our universe whereabouts is it exactly?' Christopher wants to reference heaven within his scientific framework, the **adverb** 'exactly' requiring a specific answer, which doesn't exist. Ironically, his attempt to understand separates him further from others because his fixation with the rules and boundaries of science, logic and puzzles cannot accommodate the blurry possibilities of other people's thinking, such as the existence or otherwise of heaven.

Questions

QUICK TEST
1. Why is Christopher so interested in space?
2. What does Christopher's desire to be an astronaut symbolise in the play?
3. Why are metaphors confusing to Christopher?
4. How does Christopher turn Wellington's death into a puzzle?
5. How does he use puzzles to his advantage when travelling?

EXAM PRACTICE

Using one or more of the 'Key Quotations to Learn', write a paragraph analysing the combined symbolism of science, logic and puzzles in the play.

You must be able to: understand the symbolism of maths and the Maths A-Level in the play.

What does maths mean to Christopher?

Maths is a significant companion to Christopher. One of the first pieces of information he tells us is that he knows all the prime numbers up to 7507, highlighting his ability as well as his interest.

Christopher measures the world around him in numbers where possible. He tells us that he is 'fifteen years and three months and two days', the individual coins that made up the £1.47 in his pocket when he arrived at the police station and the levels he has achieved in Tetris and their ranking.

He also knows that his father was out for two-and-a-half hours the day his mother left home, a fact presented as equal to all the others but with a subtext of far greater significance to the audience who start to piece together the truth before Christopher is told.

How does Christopher use maths to help himself?

Maths is a safe place for Christopher.

The journey to London is overwhelming for Christopher but he uses the security of numbers to insulate himself and find strength. He counts prime numbers to calm himself down and creates a rhythm to focus his mind when walking.

Why is the A-Level significant?

At fifteen, Christopher is young to be taking an A-Level, clear evidence of his difference from most other teenagers. However, in this instance, difference is an advantage. Achieving a good mark will be of real benefit to Christopher's future.

The A-Level can be seen as a celebration of Christopher's unique qualities. He is proud to tell Mrs Alexander that he is the first person in his school to do an A-Level. It feels like a denial of his ability when his mother postpones Christopher sitting the exam.

Through the A-Level, we see Ed truly appreciate Christopher as an individual, recognising both his interest and talent in maths as important. He will not accept the school's limiting view that Christopher should not be treated differently in this way.

Ed's attempt to reconcile with Christopher feels genuine when he comes to see him after the exam to ask how it went. He buys Christopher a *Further Maths for A-Level* book and tells Mrs Gascoyne that Christopher is going to take the further exam the following year.

His A-Level success symbolises Christopher's growth to independence. Not only does he have the confidence now to look for a more ambitious future but both he and the audience can see that there is potential for him to make a reality of these more ambitious aims.

Key Quotations to Learn

Ed: '... this is the one thing he is really good at.' (Part One)

Ed: 'I'm very proud of you, Christopher.' (Part Two)

Christopher: 'And I'm going to get an A*.' (Part Two)

Summary

- Christopher measures himself and the world around him through maths.
- His ability in maths is an advantageous difference to others.
- He uses maths to focus his mind and calm himself.
- Ed fights for Christopher's right to pursue his potential by taking A-Level Maths.
- Christopher's success in the exam completes his journey to independence.

Sample Analysis

Sitting the Maths A-Level creates a bridge between Christopher's difference and the everyday world. Even characters who understand Christopher well readily connect with both the idea of the exam and its outcome in a significant way. Siobhan is clearly affected by his success when she stutters 'Oh. Oh. That's just. That's terrific Christopher'. She knows many of the things that Christopher likes, such as space and red cars, but is so taken with the value of this achievement that she is lost for words, only managing a few repetitive short sentences.

Questions

QUICK TEST

1. Why does Christopher like maths?
2. How does Christopher use maths to help him?
3. Why is it important to Ed that Christopher takes the maths exam?
4. What does Christopher's success in A-Level Maths symbolise?

EXAM PRACTICE

Using one or more of the 'Key Quotations to Learn', write a paragraph analysing the symbolism of maths and the Maths A-Level for Christopher.

Animals and Policemen

You must be able to: understand the symbolism of animals and policemen in the play.

What is significant about animals?

Wellington's death is dramatic and shocking to the audience. However, whilst Christopher is concerned on discovering the dog – and the subsequent confusion starts a process of discovery for him – his initial response seems unemotional, immediately signalling some difference in his character. At the end of the play, Christopher's new dog signals the end of this troubling period.

Although he solves the puzzle of Who Killed Wellington, order is not restored until Christopher returns home with Judy and the Boones begin re-establishing their family relationships.

Christopher knows where he stands with animals. His choice of a rat for a pet may seem odd to some people, but Christopher is well-informed and knows that, unlike their disease-ridden reputation, they are clean animals.

Christopher does not talk of having any friends in the play so Toby offers him a real sense of companionship. He can express and receive love in a simple way – Toby's needs are very straightforward and Christopher looks after him well, not having to worry about interpreting his expressions or language.

What do the police symbolise to Christopher?

Policemen uphold the law and therefore represent the principle of rules. This is deeply reassuring to Christopher; rules are boundaries which, when maintained, create order. Christopher believes that policemen will act in a predictable way according to their 'rules'.

Christopher thinks he has a sense of how police systems operate, possibly through his interest in the murder mystery genre. They do not, however, record an interview with him or give him a written certificate of caution as he expects.

Ironically, it is Christopher's total adherence to the truth that really threatens to get him into trouble. He cannot **infer** the unspoken rules of his interaction at the police station where, in order to be released, he needs to suggest that he did not mean to hit the policeman.

Christopher finally feels disillusioned with the police when it seems they are attempting to return him to his father, in his mind, a dangerous man who has committed a crime.

What do the police symbolise to the audience?

The police follow due process in each instance they are required to but they are not shown as perfect examples of virtue. They get frustrated with Christopher and swear at him and he is able to outsmart their authority.

The police symbolise the complications and inconsistencies of the modern world in which even those charged with representing structure and maintaining order are not always faultless.

Key Quotations to Learn

Christopher: 'I think dogs are important too.' (Part One)

Christopher: 'Is that going to be on a piece of paper like a certificate I can keep?' (Part One)

Station Policeman: 'You are a bloody handful you are.' (Part Two)

Summary

- Structurally, the play opens with the death of one dog and closes with the arrival of a new puppy.
- Christopher appreciates animals because he does not have to struggle to understand them.
- Christopher appreciates the rules and order the police represent.
- He becomes disillusioned when it appears these rules are being used to protect his dangerous father.
- The imperfections of the police represent our worldly flaws – even systems of order can be disordered.

Sample Analysis

Christopher may be able to express affection through animals in a way that he struggles to do with humans. When the policeman arrives at the start of the play, Christopher tells him 'I was holding the dog'. He may have meant that he had lifted the dog up but the audience knows that an alternative interpretation of the **verb** 'holding' is a physical embrace. While physical contact with humans is too demanding for Christopher, he does not feel animals challenge him in ways he cannot understand and is free to enjoy the affection he usually feels inhibited from expressing.

Questions

QUICK TEST

1. Why is Christopher so intent on finding Who Killed Wellington?
2. What does the puppy symbolise at the end of the play?
3. What is surprising about some of the police behaviour?
4. How does Christopher manage to throw off the policeman who wants to take him home?

EXAM PRACTICE

Using one or more of the 'Key Quotations to Learn', write a paragraph analysing the similarities of what animals and the police represent to Christopher.

Christopher's Language

You must be able to: analyse what we learn about Christopher through his language.

Why is language significant?
Much of Christopher's character is presented through his style of speaking or the things he talks about.

What do we notice about the way Christopher speaks?
- He is direct: as Christopher does not **empathise** with other people's feelings, he will directly say things others may try to qualify or soften. He often uses short sentences and can seem abrupt as he gets straight to the point. However, he shows some awareness of his struggles to communicate when he says 'I don't do chatting'.

- He is very specific: Christopher includes many facts and statistics in his conversation. Facts are real and offer a concrete baseline for Christopher when talking. This contrasts with the need to infer what other less specific people are **implying**.

- He is formal: Christopher likes to use specific terminology – he calls his parents Mother and Father. The writer may also be using this to highlight an emotional distance between him and his parents based on his inability to emotionally connect in general.

- He is literal: Christopher says he does not understand metaphors because they don't say what they mean. The audience can also see that he does not understand the general implications of what people say. Although the station policeman's question about what he was doing there implicitly referred to the train station, Christopher responds with literal reference to sitting at the table.

- He reports information: Christopher does not use many **discourse markers** to indicate the direction of his speech. He tells us information as he processes it, often using the **conjunction** 'and' to begin each new sentence if he is reporting a scenario at length.

- He is honest: Christopher tells us that this is a quirk of his condition rather than being due to the quality of his character. Ironically, Christopher is repeatedly challenged on whether or not he is telling the truth, perhaps because the simple honesty of his responses seem so odd to others.

What does he talk about?
Much of the time Christopher is alone or trying to be alone so he is not in conversation. When he has to talk to people it is usually for practical reasons and his language is either **interrogative** or offers limited response.

He does speak more freely when he is talking about one of his interests, such as science or detecting. At these times, he uses longer sentences and more of them.

When particularly stressed, Christopher 'groans' as a way of avoiding communicating.

Key Quotations to Learn

Siobhan (speaking from Christopher's story): 'The dog was dead.' (Part One)

Siobhan (speaking from Christopher's story): 'After twelve and a half minutes a policeman arrived.' (Part One)

Siobhan (speaking from Christopher's story): 'My name is Christopher John Francis Boone.' (Part One)

Christopher: 'I always tell the truth.' (Part One)

Christopher: 'I don't do chatting.' (Part One)

Summary

- We can learn about Christopher's character from how he speaks and what he speaks about.
- He has several linguistic characteristics, many of which are linked to his Asperger's.
- Christopher's conversation is practical; he does not spend time 'chatting' with people.
- He speaks at greater length when he is talking about something he is interested in.

Sample Analysis

Christopher's emotional separation from other people can be seen through word choices, such as the reference to Mrs Alexander as a 'stranger'. This **unequivocal** statement defines Mrs Alexander as someone he does not know at all although this is the second time they have met. Indeed, the fact that she has just told him some very personal information suggests his life is not completely unknown to her. However, the emotional implications of her disclosure that his mother was having an affair are too much for Christopher to process and so he considers it 'strange', and not requiring his attention.

Questions

QUICK TEST
1. Why is Christopher's language particularly important?
2. Name one way in which he is formal.
3. In what ways does Christopher surprise people when he is talking?
4. How does his honesty sometimes fail?

EXAM PRACTICE
Using one or more of the 'Key Quotations to Learn', write a paragraph analysing how Christopher's language highlights features of his character.

Language: The People Who Talk to Christopher

You must be able to: analyse what we learn about Christopher through other people's language.

What is different between the way Christopher and the other characters use language?

In order to retain a sense of order, Christopher's language is precise and literal. Characters who do not suffer with Asperger syndrome feel less need to be so explicit.

Other characters in the play often use **figurative language** as a form of humour, or sarcasm, which they assume everyone understands. Whilst Christopher says that 'he was the apple of her eye' does not help him to imagine someone he likes, when the station policeman calls Christopher a 'little monkey', the audience readily understands that he feels Christopher is being cheeky and messing him around.

How is emotion presented through the language of others?

Punctuation is often used to indicate how the actors should present emotion in the language of other characters.

Exclamation marks show excitement when Ed is talking to Rhodri; **ellipsis** show hesitation when Ed is nervously explaining his lies to Christopher, the London policeman is struggling to find the right words to respond to Christopher or Judy is trying to avoid saying what she really means.

Many of the other characters swear, which Christopher never does. This is partly because they are less concerned about the formality of their language than Christopher. However, this is also one of the writer's methods of communicating stress to the audience. Mrs Shears opens the play swearing at Christopher about her dog and when Ed cannot see Christopher in London he swears very strongly at Roger.

The high incidence of swearing in Christopher's presence may suggest others' frustration in their interactions with him but it can seem inappropriate and shocking to the audience.

Alternatively, it may just be that Christopher reports swearing as part of a story that others would naturally edit out.

How do other characters communicate with Christopher?

Due to the interrogative nature of Christopher's communication and the brevity of his literal responses to others' questions, conversations often tend to have many exchanges.

Sometimes other characters offer short responses to Christopher when he has been talking at length on a subject they don't know much about, such as Christopher telling his father about space or telling Siobhan his theory on the prime suspect for Wellington's murder.

Key Quotations to Learn

Policeman One: 'If you try any of that monkey-business again, you little shit, I am going to seriously lose my rag.' (Part One)

Station Policeman: 'You are a prize specimen, aren't you?' (Part Two)

Drunk One: 'Come and look at this, Barry.' (Part Two)

Information: 'Are you for real?' (Part Two)

Summary

- Other characters use figurative language as an instinctive way of making their meaning clearer.
- Punctuation is used to show the emotion attached to other characters' language.
- Swearing is used to show other character's stress, which can seem shocking to the audience. This may be because they are frustrated by Christopher.
- Conversations between Christopher and other characters often have many short exchanges of questions and answers.

Sample Analysis

Characters who have never met Christopher before are often quite rude to him. Personal comments describing him as a 'bloody handful' are shocking in the first instance because of the inappropriate use of an **expletive** in the presence of a young person. However, lack of understanding of Asperger's and unwillingness to give Christopher a chance can seem quite unfair to the audience, who will feel he does not deserve such treatment. Again, Christopher's character is presented as a problem for someone else who, without understanding the specific nature of his condition, appears to feel superior enough to say things that someone else may feel more offended by.

Questions

QUICK TEST
1. How does the writer attach emotion to others' language?
2. How does the writer show other characters are stressed?
3. Why is other characters' swearing shocking to the audience?
4. Why are there often so many exchanges in Christopher's conversations with others?

EXAM PRACTICE
Using one or more of the 'Key Quotations to Learn', write a paragraph analysing how others' language highlights attitudes to Christopher.

Tips and Assessment Objectives

You must be able to: understand how to approach the exam question and meet the requirements of the mark scheme.

Quick Tips

- You will get a choice of two questions. Do the one that best matches your knowledge, the quotations you have learned and the things you have revised.

- Make sure you know what the question is asking you. Underline key words and pay particular attention to the bullet point prompts that come with the question.

- You should spend about 45 minutes on your *The Curious Incident of the Dog in the Night-Time* response. Allow yourself five minutes to plan your answer so there is some structure to your essay.

- All your paragraphs should contain a clear idea, a relevant reference to the play (ideally a quotation) and analysis of how Stephens conveys this idea. Whenever possible, you should link your comments to the play's context.

- It can sometimes help, after each paragraph, to quickly re-read the question to keep yourself focussed on the exam task.

- Keep your writing concise. If you waste time 'waffling' you won't be able to include the full range of analysis and understanding that the mark scheme requires.

- It is a good idea to remember what the mark scheme is asking of you …

AO1: Understand and respond to the play (12 marks)

This is all about coming up with a range of points that match the question, supporting your ideas with references from the play and writing your essay in a mature, academic style.

Lower	Middle	Upper
The essay has some good ideas that are mostly relevant. Some quotations and references are used to support the ideas.	A clear essay that always focusses on the exam question. Quotations and references support ideas effectively. The response refers to different points in the play.	A convincing, well-structured essay that answers the question fully. Quotations and references are well-chosen and integrated into sentences. The response covers the whole play (not everything, but ideas from both parts rather than just focussing on one or two sections).

AO2: Analyse effects of Stephens' language, form and structure (12 marks)

You need to comment on how specific words, language techniques, sentence structures, stage directions or the narrative structure allows Stephens to get his ideas across to the audience. This could simply be something about a character or a larger idea he is exploring through the play. To achieve this, you will need to have learned good quotations to analyse.

Lower	Middle	Upper
Identification of some different methods used by Stephens to convey meaning. Some subject terminology.	Explanation of Stephens' different methods. Clear understanding of the effects of these methods. Accurate use of subject terminology.	Analysis of the full range of Stephens' methods. Thorough exploration of the effects of these methods. Accurate range of subject terminology.

AO3: Understand the relationship between the play and its contexts (6 marks)

For this part of the mark scheme, you need to show your understanding of how the characters or Stephens' ideas relate to the performance of the play.

Lower	Middle	Upper
Some awareness of how ideas in the play link to its context.	References to relevant aspects of context show a clear understanding.	Exploration is linked to specific aspects of the play's contexts to show detailed understanding.

AO4: Written accuracy (4 marks)

You need to use accurate vocabulary, expression, punctuation and spelling. Although it's only four marks, this could make the difference between a lower or a higher grade.

Lower	Middle	Upper
Reasonable level of accuracy. Errors do not get in the way of the essay making sense.	Good level of accuracy. Vocabulary and sentences help to keep ideas clear.	Consistent high level of accuracy. Vocabulary and sentences are used to make ideas clear and precise.

Practice Questions

1. How is Christopher's character presented in *The Curious Incident of the Dog in the Night-Time*?

   Write about:
   - what Christopher says and does
   - how Stephens presents Christopher by the way he writes.

2. How does Stephens present Judy as a parent in *The Curious Incident of the Dog in the Night-Time*?

   Write about:
   - how Stephens presents Judy's character
   - how Stephens uses the character of Judy to explore ideas of parenthood.

3. How does Stephens present the relationship between Christopher and his father in *The Curious Incident of the Dog in the Night-Time*?

   Write about:
   - what Christopher and Ed's relationship is like
   - how Stephens presents their relationship by the way he writes.

4. How and why does Christopher change in *The Curious Incident of the Dog in the Night-Time*?

   Write about:
   - Christopher's character at the start of the play and as it progresses
   - how Stephens presents the change in Christopher by the way he writes.

5. How does Stephens use Christopher to explore issues of difference in *The Curious Incident of the Dog in the Night-Time*?

   Write about:
   - what issues of difference are presented in the play
   - how Stephens uses Christopher to explore some of these ideas.

6. How is the audience made to understand and sympathise with Christopher in *The Curious Incident of the Dog in the Night-Time*?

   Write about:
   - why the audience sympathises with Christopher
   - how Stephens helps the audience to understand Christopher's Asperger's through the way he writes.

7. How is loss presented in *The Curious Incident of the Dog in the Night-Time*?

   Write about:
   - the loss experienced in the play and its impact
   - how the characters deal with their loss.

8. It has been said that '*The Curious Incident of the Dog in the Night-Time*' is not a play about Asperger syndrome. How far do you agree with this statement?

   Write about:
   - how Asperger syndrome is presented by the way Stephens writes
   - how important Asperger syndrome is in the events of the play.

9. How is the relationship between Christopher and Siobhan presented in *The Curious Incident of the Dog in the Night-Time*?

   Write about:

- the role Christopher's relationship with Siobhan plays in his life
- how Stephens presents Christopher's relationship with Siobhan by the way he writes.

10. How is language used to help the audience understand Christopher in *The Curious Incident of the Dog in the Night-Time*?

    Write about:

    - the way Christopher speaks and what he talks about
    - the language other characters use when talking to Christopher.

11. How does Stephens present characters coming into conflict in *The Curious Incident of the Dog in the Night-Time*?

    Write about:

    - why some of the characters come into conflict
    - how Stephens presents these characters coming into conflict.

12. Through Siobhan, the audience gets a different perspective of Christopher. How important do you think this is in *The Curious Incident of the Dog in the Night-Time*?

    Write about:

    - what we learn about Christopher through Siobhan
    - how important this is in the context of the whole play.

13. At the end of the play, Christopher asks 'Does that mean I can do anything?' How far do you think it is possible for Christopher to achieve whatever he chooses at the end of *The Curious Incident of the Dog in the Night-Time*?

    Write about:

    - what Christopher's successes suggest about his ability to deal with challenge in his future

- how Stephens presents the challenges he continues to experience.

14. 'It is hard to feel sympathy for either of Christopher's parents in *The Curious Incident of the Dog in the Night-Time*.' How far do you agree with this view?

    Write about:

    - the reasons why the audience may or may not feel sorry for either of them
    - how Ed and Judy are presented by the way Stephens writes.

15. To what extent does Christopher's condition create the problems presented in *The Curious Incident of the Dog in the Night-Time*?

    Write about:

    - some of the problems created by Christopher's condition
    - how Stephens presents Christopher's condition through the way he writes.

16. 'The death of Wellington is of little significance in *The Curious Incident of the Dog in the Night-Time*.' How far do you agree with this view?

    Write about:

    - the role of Wellington and his death in the play
    - how Stephens uses Wellington's death to explore some of his ideas.

17. To what extent is communication responsible for the various outcomes in *The Curious Incident of the Dog in the Night-Time*?

    Write about:

    - different examples of communication and its impact in the play
    - how Stephens presents communication through the way he writes.

Planning a Character Question Response

You must be able to: understand what an exam question is asking you and prepare your response.

How might an exam question on character be phrased?

A typical character question will read like this:

How and why does Christopher change in *The Curious Incident of the Dog in the Night-Time*?

Write about:

- Christopher's character at the start of the play and as it progresses
- how Stephens presents the change in Christopher by the way he writes.

[30 marks + 4 AO4 marks]

How do I work out what to do?

The focus of this question is clear: Christopher and how his character changes.

'How' and 'why' are important elements of this question.

For AO1, 'how' requires you to display a clear understanding of what Christopher is like, the ways in which he changes and the reasons for these changes.

For AO2, 'how' requires you to analyse the different ways in which Stephens' use of language, structure and the dramatic form help to show the audience what Christopher is like. Ideally, you should include quotations that you have learnt but, if necessary, you can make a clear reference to a specific part of the play.

You also need to remember to link your comments to the play's context to achieve your AO3 marks and write accurately to pick up your four AO4 marks for spelling, punctuation and grammar.

How can I plan my essay?

You have approximately 45 minutes to write your essay.

This isn't long but you should spend the first five minutes writing a quick plan. This will help you to focus your thoughts and produce a well-structured essay.

Try to come up with five or six ideas. Each of these ideas can then be written up as a paragraph.

You can plan in whatever way you find most useful. Some students like to just make a quick list of points and then re-number them into a logical order. Spider diagrams are particularly popular; look at the example on the opposite page.

Opening introduction to Christopher through language: direct, factual, unemotional – 'the dog was dead' (Context: Asperger syndrome)

Success of journey = increased awareness and tolerance – 'I can't see any stars here'/'He's called Sandy'; more confidence – 'Does that mean I can do anything?'

Christopher's explicit description of his struggles in communication issues – 'I find people confusing' – compare with audience inference of behaviour – groaning

How and why Christopher changes

Challenges of the journey (link to context of performance/staging) = new responses from Christopher, 'He makes his hand into a telescope to limit his field of vision'

Narrative structure: discovery of Wellington starts change and leads to new plot/journey; 'I decided to go out on my own' – link to Struggle for Independence theme; thinking process as he writes the book

Significance of supportive relationship with Siobhan shown through reading his book; 'Is this what you want to do Christopher?'

Summary

- Make sure you know what the focus of the essay is.
- Remember to analyse how ideas are conveyed by Stephens.
- Try to relate your ideas to the play's context of performance.

Questions

QUICK TEST
1. What key skills do you need to show in your answer?
2. What are the benefits of quickly planning your essay?
3. Why do you need to have learned quotations for the exam?

EXAM PRACTICE

Plan a response to this exam question:

How and why does Judy Boone change in *The Curious Incident of the Dog in the Night-Time*?

Write about:
- the initial presentation of Judy's character
- how Stephens presents the change in Judy by the way he writes.

[30 marks + 4 AO4 marks]

How and why does Christopher change in *The Curious Incident of the Dog in the Night-Time*?

Write about:

- Christopher's character at the start of the play and as it progresses
- how Stephens presents the change in Christopher by the way he writes.

[30 marks + 4 AO4 marks]

The play opens with a dramatic scene of a dead dog. Christopher uses a reporting style to say that 'the dog was dead' in a direct and unemotional way. This gives the audience a sense of Christopher's character (1), which is maybe linked to some kind of developmental disability, probably Asperger syndrome (2).

Christopher explicitly tells the audience that 'I find people confusing'. He says that he does not understand metaphors because they don't say what they mean, which shows that he uses language in a literal way. Dramatic irony is created in the play through the difference between what Christopher tells the audience and what they can tell we understand through his behaviour, language and the way other people react to him (3). When he starts groaning and refuses to talk to the policeman, the audience can see that he is actually really stressed but does not know how to tell anyone. This is because Christopher struggles to understand and communicate emotions (4).

Christopher's change actually starts at the start of the play (5). When he hits the policeman, he is taken to the police station, which is a new setting outside of his day-to-day routine. After this, Christopher starts making decisions for himself and speaking to new people on his street to find out who killed Wellington. But when he solves the murder, a new storyline starts because he decides to travel to London to find his mother. This links to the theme of the Struggle for Independence (6).

Christopher's relationship with Siobhan is very supportive and gives Christopher stability all through the play (7). They share an intellectual connection that is symbolised by Siobhan's narration of his book. Siobhan teaches Christopher how to understand people's emotions and she is the only character who always asks Christopher genuine questions about how he feels like 'Is this what you want to do Christopher?' (8). In comparison, Ed and Judy's relationships with Christopher are flawed because of the stress of looking after him that makes them behave in selfish and irresponsible ways. Christopher's journey to London forces them to recognise his needs and take responsibility for their actions (9).

Christopher's journey forces him to deal with new situations. Stephens uses the ensemble cast to visually and audibly create the sights and sounds of the train station so the audience can experience what Christopher is feeling. When Christopher 'makes his hand into a telescope to limit his field of vision', the audience see that he still needs help to manage his environment but he is starting to create these for himself (10).

*Interestingly (11), not everything is better for Christopher in London. This is symbolised when Christopher says 'I can't see the stars here'. It is like he can't think properly, just like he can't see the stars because of the light pollution. As a result of everything he has experienced he is more tolerant of things that used to really trouble him. He names his dog 'Sandy' without thinking about the yellow and brown colours that name relates to. By the end of the play, Christopher has a new-found confidence in his abilities. He uses a **rhetorical question** 'Does that mean I can do anything?' but this does not need an answer as he can now rely on himself to create his own future (12).*

1. The first paragraph responds directly to the question using quotation for support. AO1

2. Link to context of Christopher's condition. AO3

3. Writer's dramatic techniques identified. AO2

4. Specific link to the question. AO1

5. Point about structure. AO2

6. Slightly rushed paragraph. Setting, structure, plot and theme are linked but no point is developed. Reference is made to events in the text but there is no supporting quotation or analysis. AO1/AO2

7. Although a good point is being made at the start of this paragraph, it seems disjointed from the argument of the essay so far. Use a linking phrase to create a coherent structure. AO1

8. Reasonable analysis of character using subject terminology linked to the writer's technique. AO2

9. The points being made here are not inaccurate but they lack a specific link to the question. AO1

10. Clear and well written paragraph responding to task, starting with a strong point, using appropriate support from the text and making reference to context of performance. AO1/AO3/AO4

11. Shows some 'thoughtful consideration'. AO1

12. Good use of subject terminology but the analysis is a little simplistic – an alternative interpretation would offer more depth. AO1/AO2.

Questions

EXAM PRACTICE
Choose a paragraph of this essay. Read it through a few times then try to rewrite and improve it. You might:
- Improve the sophistication of the language or the clarity of expression.
- Replace a reference with a quotation or use a better quotation.
- Ensure quotations are embedded in the sentence.
- Provide more detailed, or a wider range of, analysis.
- Use more subject terminology.
- Link some context to the analysis more effectively.

Grade 7+ Annotated Response

> A proportion of the best top-band answers will be awarded Grade 8 or Grade 9. To achieve this, you should aim for a sophisticated, fluid and nuanced response that displays flair and originality.

How and why does Christopher change in *The Curious Incident of the Dog in the Night-Time*? Write about:

- Christopher's character at the start of the play and as it progresses
- how Stephens presents the change in Christopher by the way he writes.

[30 marks + 4 AO4 marks]

*Through the first speech of the play, Mrs Shears signposts that, at least at this point, Christopher often finds himself responding to others and their misguided judgements of him (1). He says he 'finds people confusing' and, indeed (2), is 'frozen to the spot' (3) by her aggressive accusations and expletives that would seem quite shocking to the audience. Perhaps (4) Stephens is advising us that at the start of the play Christopher is stuck in time, metaphorically trapped within the limiting symptoms of his Asperger syndrome (5), or the limits of others' understanding of it. However (6), the death of Wellington invades Christopher's daily routine and instigates a chain reaction of change. Christopher declares an emerging ability to both think and take action by himself through the strength of the personal **pronoun** and choice of verb in 'I decided to go out on my own' when he decides to investigate Wellington's murder against his father's instructions.*

*Siobhan is integral to the start of the play, showing her intellectual support for Christopher by reading aloud from his book. She also introduces a key structural feature of the narrative that moves between the present action and Christopher's accounts in his book (7). She narrates (7) his initial factual statement that 'the dog was dead', the **alliteration** of which also highlights its brevity. This is direct and unemotional, typical of someone who struggles to empathise with others or understand their feelings, but it does not evidence the stress we actually see Christopher experience on stage (8) as he resorts to 'groaning' to avoid communicating at all. Stephens builds this dramatic irony in the gap between what Christopher tells us and what we are able to infer from his behaviours and others' reactions (8).*

Siobhan remains a stable influence on Christopher throughout the play. One of the features of Christopher's change is his ability to make decisions for himself in which we can see Siobhan's clear influence. Even when about to sit his maths exam, the culmination of all his efforts and the greatest symbol of independent ability (9), she asks 'Is this what you want to do Christopher?' Her selfless use of the second person and her personalised focus specifically on him encourages Christopher to think for himself whilst the verb choice 'want' makes clear that he has the power to choose his own destiny (10).

The audience are included in the physical and emotional challenges of Christopher's journey to London through the ensemble's recreation of the overwhelming sights and sounds he experiences.

Christopher has very specific interests, such as maths and science, so in a sense his 'field of vision' has always been somewhat 'limited'. However, when he makes a telescope with his own hand he metaphorically creates the tools with which he can see further and with far greater focus. In contrast, his great hopes for a new life in London providing a clean resolution to his problems are dashed by 'pollution' blocking his 'stars' (11).

Christopher's various 'investigations' identify the struggle within himself to awaken to his own potential. Sandy's yellow and brown connotations highlight that what was once so troubling now provides a new source of hope. However, while his final rhetorical question 'Does that mean I can do anything?' suggests he believes he can, we hear no response in support from Siobhan, creating a final moment of doubt for the audience to answer (12).

1. Clear focus on the start of the play establishing a strong point in response to the question. Introduces idea of **miscommunication** linked to Christopher's condition. AO1/AO3

2. Phrasing shows 'confidence' linked to top band level 6. AO1

3. Good link between quotes from different parts of the play shows a 'conceptualised response'. AO1

4. Alternative interpretation fits level 6 as 'critical/exploratory'. AO1

5. Early contextual reference of Asperger syndrome linked to Christopher's character. AO3

6. Comparative connective establishes change in response to the question. AO1

7. Critical link made between character and structure, which also references performance. AO2/AO3

8. Writer's methods/performance linked to impact on audience. AO2/AO3

9. Relevant subordinate clause provides additional information in a concise fashion: sophisticated language use. AO1/AO4

10. Conclusive point in response to question supported with word-level analysis. AO1/AO2

11. Tracking the text is conceptualised and creates a sense of argument. AO1

12. Concluding statement sums up argument in response to question with supportive links to the end of the play. AO1/AO2.

> ## Questions
>
> EXAM PRACTICE
> Spend 45 minutes writing an answer to the following question:
> How and why does Judy Boone change in *The Curious Incident of the Dog in the Night-Time*?
> Write about:
> - the initial presentation of Judy's character
> - how Stephens presents the change in Judy by the way he writes.
> [30 marks + 4 AO4 marks]
> Remember to use the plan you have already prepared.

Planning a Theme Question Response

You must be able to: understand what an exam question is asking you and prepare your response.

How might an exam question on theme be phrased?

A typical theme question will read like this:

How does Stephens present attitudes towards difference in *The Curious Incident of the Dog in the Night-Time?*

Write about:

• what some of the attitudes towards difference are

• how Stephens presents some of the attitudes by the way he writes.

[30 marks + 4 AO4 marks]

How do I work out what to do?

The focus of this question is clear: attitudes towards difference.

'What' and 'how' are important elements of this question.

For AO1, 'what' requires you to display a clear understanding of what Christopher is like, the ways in which he changes and the reasons for these changes.

For AO2, 'how' requires you to analyse the different ways in which Stephens' use of language, structure and the dramatic form help these attitudes. Ideally, you should include quotations that you have learnt but, if necessary, you can make a clear reference to a specific part of the play.

You also need to remember to link your comments to the play's context to achieve your AO3 marks and write accurately to pick up your four AO4 marks for spelling, punctuation and grammar.

How can I plan my essay?

You have approximately 45 minutes to write your essay.

This isn't long but you should spend the first five minutes writing a quick plan. This will help you to focus your thoughts and produce a well-structured essay.

Try to come up with five or six ideas. Each of these ideas can then be written up as a paragraph.

You can plan in whatever way you find most useful. Some students like to just make a quick list of points and then re-number them into a logical order. Spider diagrams are particularly popular; look at the example on the opposite page.

Strange and confusing: strangers find Christopher's behaviour odd/he doesn't understand them

Stage directions: *'For a while the two look at one another, neither entirely sure what to say or quite believing what has just happened'*

(Context: Asperger syndrome)

Attitudes towards difference

Something to be valued: Ed arguing to take Maths A-Level – 'this is the one thing he's really good at' – and making a project – 'this is more important than anything else'

Challenging: Judy sees this as personal and 'couldn't take it any more'/Ed – 'we're not exactly low maintenance, are we?' (**inclusive** language)

Not different at all: Mrs Alexander treats Christopher the same as her grandson and respects him as an individual – 'I'm not a stranger, Christopher'

Easily dismissed: Judy – 'It's only an exam', Mrs Gascoyne – 'then everybody would want to be treated differently' (writer's comment on societal social point of view)

Not real/something to make fun of: drunk men on train – 'he could be our elf mascot', information lady – 'are you for real?'/Mr Wise laughs at his joke about Christopher (Context: travelling beyond limitations of Swindon)

Summary

- Make sure you know what the focus of the essay is.
- Remember to analyse how ideas are conveyed by Stephens.
- Try to relate your ideas to the play's context of performance.

Questions

QUICK TEST

1. What key skills do you need to show in your answer?
2. What are the benefits of quickly planning your essay?
3. Why do you need to have learned quotations for the exam?

EXAM PRACTICE

Plan a response to this exam question:

How does Stephens present attitudes towards family in *The Curious Incident of the Dog in the Night-Time*?

Write about:

- what some of the attitudes towards family are
- how Stephens presents some of the attitudes by the way he writes.

[30 marks + 4 AO4 marks]

Grade 5 Annotated Response

How does Stephens present attitudes towards difference in *The Curious Incident of the Dog in the Night-Time?*

Write about:

- what some of the attitudes towards difference are
- how Stephens presents some of the attitudes by the way he writes.

[30 marks + 4 AO4 marks]

Christopher's differences are the result of having a developmental disorder called Asperger syndrome (1). In Part One, Christopher says 'I find people confusing'. This is interesting as it suggests he feels others are different to him although people might think that the play is only about Christopher being different to everyone else (2). Stephens highlights this in the stage directions (3) when Christopher hits the policeman, 'For a while the two look at one another, neither entirely sure what to say or quite believing what has just happened' (4). In this quote (5), the policeman and Christopher are the same because they both think the other one has done something wrong. But when we look at it from the outside it is easy to see the situation from Christopher's point of view – he would think it is not normal to be grabbed by someone so it is right to defend yourself.

This links to the setting of the National Theatre production that tries to present the story as though the audience are inside Christopher's mind (6). The company interacts with Christopher using **physical theatre** *to show his imaginative way of thinking. There is no set but the stage looks as though it is graph paper, which Christopher draws out his thoughts on using equations and puzzles. From this point of view, it is easier for the audience to understand Christopher's behaviours, even though their greater awareness of the social world means they also recognise the impact Christopher has on others in ways which he cannot. This is called dramatic irony (7).*

Judy loves Christopher and does not make fun of him but she still struggles to take his needs seriously and says his Maths A-Level is 'only an exam'. She doesn't take the time to recognise how important this exam is to Christopher. It is an area of interest for him and it represents an opportunity for him to do something independent. Worse than this (8), Mrs Gascoyne actually seems quite threatened that should Christopher pursue his unique talents 'then everyone would want to be treated differently' as though this is not acceptable or she can't manage it, even though she runs a school for students with special needs.

Linked to this (8), part of the reason why Judy left is because she 'couldn't take it anymore' and even though she says Ed is more patient than her when looking after Christopher he says 'we're not exactly low maintenance' like Christopher is some sort of machine that needs to be serviced (9). This idea that somehow Christopher's difference means he's not human is also shown by the information lady in London who asks him if he is 'for real?' and the drunk men on the train who say that

Christopher can be their 'elf mascot'. They are making fun of him but they are also suggesting that being different to them means that Christopher's value has been reduced to no more than a puppet (10).

In the end, we see that Christopher is valued deeply whether this is anything to do with his differences or not. Ed does show his appreciation of Christopher's difference by doing something Christopher would like and making a 'project' out of their attempts to rebuild their relationship. He uses a superlative statement (11) that 'this is more important than anything else', which suggests that he just wants to be close to his son again.

1. Strong statement putting the focus of the question in context. AO3.

2. Analytical point that creates a sense of argument. AO1

3. Point linked to writer's methods. AO2

4. Good choice of textual reference but it would be better to embed it within the sentence. AO1

5. Simplistic to refer to a piece of evidence as a 'quote'. AO1

6. Contextualised reference to performance. AO3

7. This is accurate but it is not particularly analytical just to spot techniques. Better to analyse why a writer uses a particular method using supporting evidence. AO2

8. Linking phrases attempt to create sense of a developing argument. AO1

9. Evidence taken from different parts of the text and different characters helps build a critical response to the question. AO1

10. Series of connected ideas analysed at word level. AO2

11. Specific subject terminology. AO2

Questions

EXAM PRACTICE

Choose a paragraph of this essay. Read it through a few times then try to rewrite and improve it. You might:

- Improve the sophistication of the language or the clarity of expression.
- Replace a reference with a quotation or use a better quotation.
- Ensure quotations are embedded in the sentence.
- Provide more detailed, or a wider range of, analysis.
- Use more subject terminology.
- Link some context to the analysis more effectively.

A proportion of the best top-band answers will be awarded Grade 8 or Grade 9. To achieve this, you should aim for a sophisticated, fluid and nuanced response that displays flair and originality.

How does Stephens present attitudes towards difference in *The Curious Incident of the Dog in the Night-Time*?

Write about:

- what some of the attitudes towards difference are
- how Stephens presents some of the attitudes by the way he writes.

[30 marks + 4 AO4 marks]

In Part One, Christopher subverts the idea that he is the one who is different by asserting that other people are 'confusing' to him (1). He does not realise that in 'finding' them as such, he has implied that the business of knowing one another in this play is a process of discovery in which characters search for and uncover meaning in one another (2).

*Christopher's differences to others are readily understood as a result of his Asperger syndrome and the associated behaviours easily recognised (3). As such, the National Theatre production of the play attempts to present the world instead from Christopher's point of view (4). The audience is brought into Christopher's imagination through elements of physical theatre used to enact events from the past and co-construct with Christopher his thoughts and plans as they are developing. We even experience his challenges such as the multiple voices presenting all the information available in the train station, creating an inescapable moment of uncomfortable **sensory** stress.*

However, Christopher's understanding of the social world is limited in comparison to the audience, creating dramatic irony in the difference between what he knows and what we understand (5). For example, when Christopher hits the policeman: 'For a while the two look at one another, neither entirely sure what to say or quite believing what has just happened' (6). At the same time, the pair are made equal by the inclusive statement 'the two', both finding the other inconceivably strange and at fault, the idea of difference is symbolised within their stand-off.

In fact, Judy says she left because she 'couldn't take it anymore', the verb 'take' suggesting she felt the stresses were personal, as though Christopher was deliberately giving her problems. Her inability to see beyond her own experience means that she struggles to find value in the qualities his difference brings. To her, it is 'only an exam' because the adverb 'only' has a singular tone that focusses her own perspective without recognising the incredible opportunities an exam offers Christopher and that, in this instance, Christopher's difference is a significant source of strength (7).

Equally so, Mrs Gascoyne cannot see further than the problems difference could create. Ironically, in her attempts to control Christopher's individuality she is rather inclusive in suggesting that 'everyone' has the potential to be different, which seems very threatening to her. Although to her, being different is about the way you need to be 'treated' rather than how you want to behave (8). Stephens is likely using Mrs Gascoyne to present society's general view but as it is hard to look upon her perspective favourably in this scene, we can assume he doesn't agree with it (9).

In contrast (10), Stephens uses Mrs Alexander to show that despite his difference, Christopher can be treated in a very 'normal' way as she makes comparisons between him and her grandson as though he is like any other teenager. However (11), the fact that it is Christopher who maintains their distance by continuing to see her as someone 'strange' to him suggests that it takes more than good intentions to unite differences. Ed's relationship with Christopher suffers through seeing it as a practical form of 'maintenance' and it is only when he removes the difference by seeing life through Christopher's eyes and creating a 'project', which they both can share, because 'it is more important than anything else', that the connection is restored.

1. Initial reference to Christopher's Asperger's. AO3
2. Introduction seeks to create a point of view to be developed. AO1
3. Contextualising the theme of the question. AO3
4. Alternative context of performance provided. AO3
5. Dramatic device used to support a thematic point. AO2
6. Evidence naturally embedded in writing. AO1
7. Different evidence linked to support and extension of point helps develop the argument. AO1
8. Deconstructing and analysing evidence at word level. AO2
9. Writer's point of view. AO3
10. Alternative perspective meets 'exploratory' definition in top band. AO1
11. Alternative interpretation avoids simplistic conclusions. AO1

> ## Questions
>
> EXAM PRACTICE
> Spend 45 minutes writing an answer to the following question:
>
> How does Stephens present attitudes towards family in *The Curious Incident of the Dog in the Night-Time*?
>
> Write about:
> * what some of the attitudes towards family are
> * how Stephens presents some of the attitudes by the way he writes.
> [30 marks + 4 AO4 marks]
>
> Remember to use the plan you have already prepared.

Glossary

Action – the events and things that are done as part of the plot.

Adjective – a word that describes a noun.

Adverb – a word that describes a verb.

Alliteration – a series of words beginning with the same letter or sound.

Articulate – speaking fluently in a way that makes sense.

Asperger syndrome – a developmental disorder on the autism spectrum.

Atmosphere – the mood or emotion in a play.

Cacophony/cacophonous – a harsh mixture of sounds that do not work well together.

Characteristic – typical of a particular person, place or thing.

Chronological – following the order of occurrence.

Company – a group of actors, singers or dancers who perform together.

Conjunction – a word that links clauses together in a sentence (such as: and, but, yet).

Coping mechanism – methods by which stress or challenge is managed.

Continuous – carrying on without interruption.

Developmental disability – a range of symptoms or conditions that impair an individual's progress.

Devise – a process of creating physical performance.

Dialogue – a conversation between two or more people.

Direct – without intervening factors.

Direct address – name of the person who is being spoken directly to.

Discourse marker – a word or phrase that organises discourse into sections.

Dramatic irony – when the audience of a play is aware of something that a character on stage is not aware of.

Ellipsis – a series of three dots that indicate the omission of a set of words.

Empathise – ability to understand and share someone else's feelings.

Emphatic – clear and insistent expression.

Enact – to put into practice an idea or word.

Ensemble – a group of musicians, actors or dancers who perform together.

Environment – the surroundings of a person or place.

Expletive – a swear word.

Explicit – a clear and direct expression of meaning.

Fictional – a made up story.

Figurative language – words or expressions with meaning different to literal interpretation.

First person – the viewpoint of a character writing or speaking about themselves.

Flashback – a dramatic device showing events in the past.

Foreshadow – a hint at future events in the play.

Formal – keeping with convention.

Implicit/implication/implicitly/implying – suggested meaning.

Inclusive – involving all relevant parties.

Infer – to deduce or conclude from something suggested rather than explicitly stated.

Initiative – independently taking charge.

Interpretation – an understanding or explanation of something.

Interrogative – a question.

Investigation – carry out an inquiry or examine the facts to establish the truth.

Ironic – unexpected; happening in contrast to what is expected, sometimes as a source of amusement.

Literal – the exact meaning of something.

Metaphor – a descriptive technique using comparison to say one thing is something else.

Miscommunication – failure to communicate adequately.

Modal verb – a verb which describes the probability or certainty of something e.g. could, might, will, must.

Monologue – one person speaking at length.

Narrative – the telling of a story.

Narrator/narration – the person telling or the act of telling a story.

Noun – an object or thing.

Objective – a thing aimed for or sought after.

Pace – development at a particular speed.

Parameter – a boundary that defines a particular activity or idea.

Pattern – a regular sequence.

Perspective – a point of view or way of seeing something.

Physical theatre – a form of theatre that emphasises physical movement as the main method of expression.

Plural – more than one.

Practical – concerned with doing something rather than just thinking about it.

Precise – exact and accurate expression.

Pre-recorded – recorded prior to the present.

Pronoun – a word that takes the place of a noun (such as: I, she, them, it).

Reflective/reflections – characterised by deep thought or thoughts looking into the past.

Represents/representative – be a symbol for.

Rhetorical question – a question asked to create thought, not necessarily requiring an answer.

Rhythm – a regular repetitive pattern of image, movement or sound.

Sensory – related to the physical senses.

Sequencing – arrange in a particular order.

Set – the physical design on stage, often used to create the setting.

Setting – a place where action happens.

Signifies – a sign of something or makes something known.

Simile – comparing one thing with another of a different kind, usually for emphasis.

Solitary – single or alone.

Stage direction – instructions given by the writer for how aspects of the play should be performed.

Strategies – plans of action designed to have specific outcomes.

Subtext – a suggestion or implication not directly stated.

Symbol/symbolise – when something (object, colour, word, place) represents a specific idea or meaning.

Tableau – where the actors freeze their action to represent a specific idea.

Tension – a feeling of anticipation, discomfort or excitement.

Trial – a test of the performance, quality or suitability of someone or something.

Unequivocal – leaving no doubt.

Verb – a doing or action word.

Visualise – imagine or form a mental image.

Answers

Pages 4–5
1. Wellington was killed with a garden fork.
2. He likes dogs and thinks they are important as well as humans.
3. They do a lot of talking without using words and they talk using metaphors.
4. She went into hospital and then had a heart attack.
5. He has a good relationship with Siobhan, who helps him to understand the world and find ways to function appropriately in it.

Exam Practice

Answers should focus on the details Christopher includes when writing his story, the way he writes and his responses to situations.

Analysis could discuss the difference between what Christopher tells the audience and what they understand as a result. The short length of Christopher's sentences highlight a specific and factual interpretation of the world. His limited use of words offers no opportunity for reflective consideration, which indicates a narrow emotional range. He is unaware that this can seem odd to others, identifying his difficulty interacting with people. The choice of quote spoken by Siobhan gives some sense of how well she understands him and how he allows her to help him engage with the world.

Pages 6–7
1. She knows that he lives at number 36 and she sees him travelling to school on the bus.
2. He was close to Wellington and divorced Mrs Shears.
3. Not to speak to anyone about who killed the dog, not to go into people's gardens and not to carry on with his detective game.
4. That he is not aware of his mother's affair.

Exam Practice

Answers should include a range of responses to Christopher, from not knowing about his condition, not fully understanding his needs or showing insensitivity towards them to treating Christopher with respect and trying to help him.

Analysis could focus on the verb choice 'laughs' and Rhodri's rhetorical question, which both assume a position of superiority to Christopher on the basis of his difference. The pronoun 'you' shows the comment is directed at Ed and the expletive 'God' implies a link to frustration, possibly expressed by Ed in private; 'third degree' is insensitively ironic as Christopher would not understand the metaphor, isolating him further from the conversation.

Pages 8–9
1. She would be living a country life with a local man in the south of France.
2. He was looking for his book that his father had taken.
3. She was lonely because her and Ed no longer talked, she felt Christopher was calmer with Ed and that everyone would be better off if she was not there.
4. Ed killed Wellington because he thought he might get together with Mrs Shears after Judy left but she rejected him.
5. Christopher reasons that as he killed Wellington, Ed could kill him as well.

Exam Practice

Analysis will notice that the pace of changing events is highlighted by Christopher's discoveries being made within the short time it has taken him to write this section of the book. The 'mystery' has seemed like a puzzle with no emotional

implications for Christopher until Ed personally insults him with his sarcastic alliteration. He creates a division between them with the pronoun 'you're' in contrast to Judy's inclusive use of the **plural** pronoun 'us' later. Christopher's final short sentence decisively ends the chaos, indicating some ability to take control that he develops in Part Two.

Pages 10–11
1. He walks in a progressively increasing spiral until he comes across it.
2. He is trying to persuade him to get off the train when it starts moving.
3. He hides in the luggage rack.
4. He speaks to the lady at the information counter.
5. The normal series of events one undertakes to travel are sequentially and extensively detailed, creating a sense of magnitude. The cacophony of pre-recorded voices overwhelm the audience, obliging them to absorb every piece of information alongside Christopher.

Exam Practice

Answers should include a full range of challenges, focussing on the situation being new and overwhelming for Christopher.

Analysis might focus on the behaviours of other people as well as of Christopher. The intellectual link between Siobhan and Christopher is highlighted by her intuitive appearance in contrast to the incredulous question of the woman at the information counter. Christopher uncharacteristically imagines support for himself by identifying with a dog whilst the isolation of his reality is shown through his solitary position on stage.

Pages 12–13
1. She is very upset and then she is angry.
2. As Christopher wants to stay there and Judy says he can, there is nothing for him to do.
3. He is scared of Mr Shears.
4. They are for children.
5. He says he never thinks about anyone other than himself.

Exam Practice

Answers should focus on both the practical and emotional issues Christopher's arrival raises for Judy as well as Ed and Roger's reactions to the situation.

Analysis could include the verb 'howl', which is an animal-like, painful noise, reminding the audience of Wellington and suggesting a metaphoric link to Judy's 'death' for the past two years. The increased use of swearing by multiple characters highlights raised tensions and there is an implicit threat unspoken in Judy's ellipsis. The **noun** 'contribution' betrays Roger's lack of interest and the verb 'appreciated' inappropriately demands attention, although Christopher is the person most at need. Judy's dismissive 'only' suggests an inability to compromise her own needs for Christopher.

Pages 14–15
1. She says that killing Wellington is just a little crime and that Mrs Shears will have to press charges in order for the police to arrest Ed.
2. He has to use the same toilet as other people.
3. He died because he was very old for a rat.
4. She is not his mother.
5. Sandy sleeps on Christopher's bed with him when Christopher stays at his father's house.

Exam Practice

Answers should include the various resolutions: Christopher and Judy's return home; Christopher taking the maths exam; Ed's attempts to rebuild his relationship with Christopher.

Analysis might focus on Ed and Judy's inclusive use of 'we're' and 'let's' and Ed's use of the subject-specific noun 'project', highlighting their intention to take Christopher's needs seriously and to work with him. 'Sandy' could be seen as a mix of yellow and brown, Christopher's two least favourite colours but of less significance now that he has managed to handle far greater challenges. The rhetorical question at the end, although unanswered, shows a more independent Christopher seeking his own solutions.

Pages 16–17
1. Siobhan is used as a narrator of Christopher's book. In between moments of action regarding the Wellington

plot, she reads aloud some of his reflections, memories and experiences of having Asperger's.

2. The flashbacks and memories show us some of Christopher's past. In other places, Christopher acts out a scene as though it is in the present even while Siobhan narrates sections indicating that it has already happened.

3. Christopher solves the mystery of Who Killed Wellington at the end of Part One meaning he has no real reason to continue writing his book. The process of this discovery, however, leads him down a new path of finding his mother.

4. He discovers Who Killed Wellington at the end of Part One and sets out to find his mother at the start of Part Two.

5. Siobhan suggests that Christopher's book is turned into a play and acted out at school.

Exam Practice

Answers should include the movement between Christopher's action and Siobhan's narration, flashbacks and memories, the new direction of the narrative and the play within a play.

Analysis could focus on Siobhan's narration of Christopher's book – the positive language and the personal **direct address** emphasises the closeness of their relationship and her role in converting it to a play highlights the impact of their intellectual connection. The adjective 'exciting' objectively describes Christopher's writing as he is not connected to the story, highlighted by the flashback from which he is physically removed by time and to which he remains unemotional, unlike the pronoun 'I', which puts him at the centre of the action when he decides to travel to London.

Pages 18–19

1. They create the setting and quick scene changes.

2. When he arrives in London on the train and is still hiding in the luggage rack.

3. That Christopher is separate from other people, in his own world.

4. They crowd him like the crowds in London.

5. Siobhan is the main person who helped him write it.

Exam Practice

Answers should include the use of the ensemble cast to play different roles, create the setting and keep the pace of the play moving quickly. They also remind the audience that Christopher's book is a play within the play they are watching.

Analysis could focus on how the ensemble can be seen both to support Christopher but also symbolise his separation from the people around him. As Christopher does not use or understand figurative language, the **simile** in the stage directions highlights that he is not aware of the company around him. Their 'cheer' may also represent the support available to Christopher that he is unable to acknowledge. He maintains the narrow focus of his day-to-day life, while they visually and audibly recreate the stress Christopher feels, giving the audience the opportunity to share his experience.

Pages 20–21

1. Asperger syndrome is on the autism spectrum. It is a developmental disability.

2. Difficulty understanding facial expressions and others' language, recognising emotion or empathising with feelings; dislike of physical contact; literal, precise and direct manner of speaking with a focus on facts; specific interests; very sensitive to sensory input; dislikes change in routine.

3. He likes maths and science.

4. Judy was upset by Christopher's extreme sensitivity to external stimulation in the shopping mall and she gets stressed by his persistent questions. Ed finds Christopher's literal responses to his questions frustrating and seems overwhelmed by Christopher's informative monologues about space.

Exam Practice

Answers should link the choice of quotes to Christopher's dislike of physical contact and his interest in maths and the fact that his disorder creates extra work and stress for his family.

Analysis would consider that even while displaying all of the key symptoms of Asperger's, Christopher is not completely unable to interact with others, using modifications to do so. Ed's adverbial phrase 'not exactly' symbolically demonstrates the conflict between the messiness of their reality and Christopher's need for precise order. Judy also talks of what she could 'not' take, each of them highlighting their perceived negative implications of trying to look after Christopher.

Pages 22–23

1. He does not travel far beyond his house and garden, school or local shops, probably because he does not like unfamiliar places.

2. Through his investigations he meets more people and starts to make independent decisions.

3. There are too many unfamiliar sights and sounds and numbers of people.

4. His presence causes Judy practical stress, there is friction with Roger and he struggles to let go of his attachments to Swindon such as his relationship with Siobhan and his maths exam.

5. He learns to tolerate less than ideal circumstances. He also knows he is capable of independently achieving significant things.

Exam Practice

Answers should focus on Christopher's familiarity with the limited parameters of his day-to-day life in comparison to feeling overwhelmed by his exposure to the world beyond Swindon.

Analysis could include the verb 'limit', which highlights Christopher's attempts to control his environment. The light pollution in London means he can't see the 'stars', which may be a symbol of London's imperfection and signifies Christopher being unable to clearly understand his new situation. 'I don't like' is a fair expression of having to tolerate waiting for his results but does not undermine his new-found sense of possibility, shown through the **emphatic** verb 'I can'.

Pages 24–25

1. First person.

2. Dialogue and action, guided by stage directions.

3. The ensemble cast can recreate his memories and act out his reflections. They interact with him, constructing visual images of his thoughts.

4. The ensemble cast communicate meaning with the audience that Christopher does not understand.

Exam Practice

Analysis could focus on the verb 'watch' and adjective 'waiting', both of which signal that the pace of the play is driven by Christopher and highlight the first person narrative of his book. 'Dare to speak' suggests an **atmosphere** of tension that the ensemble help create through their silent observation. The verb 'assembled' details the physical process by which the sets are created on stage but also the mental process of Christopher remembering incidents as he writes his book. Ed is isolated by the pronoun 'nobody'. As the company support the presentation of Christopher's thoughts, it is important to him that Ed is signalled clearly as the bad guy.

Pages 26–27

1. He cannot tell lies.

2. When Mrs Alexander alludes to Judy's affair.

3. By the end of the play he is more confident in his own abilities, he is more tolerant of things that previously caused him distress, he is more aware of the differences between himself and others and the impact of his behaviour on others.

4. Christopher represents an experience of being different from the norms of society. Through his struggle to manage this, he highlights the need for everyone to try harder to behave appropriately.

Exam Practice

Answers should recognise that Christopher's character is presented through his language and his actions, some of which happens as live action and some of which is narrated from his book.

Analysis could focus on Christopher's prioritisation of knowledge through his verb choice. His impressive accumulation of facts is ironic when his own life has very narrow boundaries. The use of 'mother' is formal, the short sentence is factual and unemotional. There is subtext in Ed's ellipsis, which suggests something not being said and this foreshadows our later discovery that Judy's problem was that she no longer loved him.

Pages 28–29

1. Christopher's Asperger's and the desertion of his wife.

2. He shouts and rants, using many back-to-back questions that are overwhelming.

3. He holds up his hand in a fan, he tells Christopher.

4. He has to be more considerate of Christopher's emotional needs, taking his time to repair the relationship and doing so in a way that is appropriate to Christopher.

Exam Practice

Answers should highlight both the positive qualities of Ed and the way he relates to Christopher, as well as those that don't reflect on him so well.

Analysis could focus on the verb 'stares', which suggests either disbelief or an absence of thought, both highlighting the differences between Ed and his son. His repeated expletives show his stress in connection to Christopher's interest in the dog. He takes new approaches at the end of the play to engage more meaningfully with Christopher, using direct language and showing respect by asking whether he can talk to him rather than assuming he can.

Pages 30–31

1. She hoped things would get easier at home and talked of a fantasy life in the French countryside.

2. She struggled to cope with Christopher, getting easily overwhelmed and angry. She felt that Ed was more patient with him and that Christopher was calmer when he and Ed were together.

3. She tries to maintain contact; she respects his right to an explanation; she asks about him in her letters; she holds up her hand like a fan to show her feelings; she leaves Roger and starts a new life with Christopher.

4. She needs to be more mindful of Christopher's needs and not put hers before his or take out her stress on him.

Exam Practice

Answers might focus on the various introductions we have to Judy before we even meet her. There is a sense of romance in her wistful longings, both in Christopher's memory and in her letters, which is juxtaposed with the reality of first seeing her mid-argument with Roger.

Analysis could focus on the verb 'wanted', which puts Judy's needs first, linked to the noun 'dream' that betrays a simplistic desire to escape her responsibilities. The verb 'used to' shows that she is more available to look after Christopher when they meet again. The verb 'howl' is animalistic, expressing the instinctive grief of her loss and suggesting that she is indeed a 'good mother'.

Pages 32–33

1. It is not relevant – she only exists in relation to Christopher and is part of the boundaries she teaches Christopher to learn.

2. Stephens interchanges Christopher's accounts of events with Siobhan's narration from Christopher's book.

3. She is a live presence on stage, as though in his mind, giving him coping mechanisms to manage himself.

4. She is his teacher not his parent.

Exam Practice

Answers could consider Siobhan's intellectual abilities as a teacher being closer to Christopher's than his parents. Their connection also comes through the distance she offers from the family problems; our lack of knowledge about Siobhan allows the focus to stay on Christopher.

Analysis could highlight 'Siobhan says' as though a statement of fact, Christopher's metaphoric stamp of approval of her input. 'Lots of different things' indicates the quality of her input, his retention of which also highlights his regard for what she says. The adjective 'sad' is emotional and distinct from most other characters' interaction with Christopher. The inclusive use of 'we' symbolises her input to the book and the co-construction of the play on stage.

Pages 34–35

1. She has a grandson Christopher's age.

2. That she had an affair with Mr Shears.

3. She shouts and swears at him and implies he has harmed her dog.

4. While he does make some concessions to Christopher staying with them, these seem half-hearted and insincere. He seems a poor comparison to Ed, both as partner and father, whatever Ed's flaws.

Exam Practice

Answers should observe that Christopher's relationships with the supporting characters both demonstrate his struggles to interact with a world beyond the safe limits of home or school and his ability to do so.

Analysis could highlight that Mrs Alexander repeatedly emphasises her reliability by negating the word 'stranger', suggesting also that Christopher is not strange to her, by using personal address and describing herself as a friend. This contrasts to Mrs Shears' impersonal and possessive command. Mr Shears' repetition of 'you' puts the blame on Christopher, while his emphasis on the verb 'think' and the adjective 'clever' suggest that he feels threatened by Christopher's abilities.

Pages 36–37

1. He sticks to the same routine and mostly only moves between home and school.

2. Christopher's discovery of Wellington.

3. Through detecting, he discovers the letters that force Ed's confession about Wellington. When Christopher leaves, he has to face the consequences of these bad decisions and attempt to make amends.

4. Despite feeling stressed by the situation, she makes personal sacrifices to take action on Christopher's behalf.

Exam Practice

Answers could observe that the change in circumstances by the end of the play reunites the family and obliges them to find ways to work well together to meet everyone's needs.

Analysis could interpret Ed's ellipsis as hesitancy, revealing an attempt to take the honest approach he is expressing. Judy's inclusive use of 'we're' proves there is a collective outcome to focussing her attention on Christopher's needs. Christopher rightly takes credit for 'solving' the mystery that resulted in all this change.

Pages 38–39

1. Christopher has specific likes and dislikes, a need for routine and can be easily overwhelmed by things that don't bother other people. All of this needs to be accommodated by anyone looking after him.

2. If she allows him a specific concession, others may feel entitled to ask for what they want too.

3. It seems easy to ridicule or abuse difference, although there are positive instances where characters either disregard others' difference or try to help it.

4. Ed kills a dog.

Exam Practice

Answers should recognise that the play is not about Asperger syndrome but uses Christopher's experience of the condition as a way of presenting ideas about difference in general. Answers might consider 'how different is different'? And does it matter? Christopher is not exempt from the universal themes of relationships and loss and his experiences allow the audience to consider another perspective. Being different does not mean being less equal – Christopher is entitled to the same care and respect as anyone else and must also offer it to others where possible.

Analysis could highlight that people choose what they consider to be different. The drunk men objectify Christopher and he judges others based on their intelligence, whereas Mrs Alexander attempts to see Christopher's point of view.

Pages 40–41

1. Two – Wellington and Toby.

2. Christopher's initial response is to ask questions but Ed tells him that this is not the time. As a result, Christopher's general lack of emotion means there is no protracted grieving period.

3. The two years without contact between each other has just been a pointless waste of time.

4. Christopher is more experienced by the end of the play – his emerging independence can be seen as an appropriate loss of childhood innocence for a teenage boy.

Exam Practice

Answers could consider that the attempt to avoid dealing

with loss often creates suffering and further loss. The denial of Judy's departure limits the depth of relationship Ed can have with his son, necessitates Judy's isolation from Christopher and results in Christopher leaving home.

Analysis should highlight that the focus of Christopher is factual, seeking explicit information to understand the situation and denying any opportunity for emotion. In contrast, Ed's metaphor 'bottling up' implicitly suggests that he has been storing his feelings. The repetition of the personal pronoun, the negative phrasing and the ellipsis suggests that Judy is overwhelmed and at a loss for words.

Pages 42–43

1. He doesn't understand their non-verbal communication or use of metaphors.
2. It makes Christopher seem blunt and offensive in ways other people would seek to avoid or soften.
3. Siobhan – as a teacher and role model.
4. She tells him the truth.

Exam Practice

Answers might include the opening scene, which makes it clear that there is a struggle to communicate effectively in this play. Wellington's death is a clear but inappropriate expression of rage, symbolising the non-verbal ways the characters often choose to demonstrate the feelings they find difficult to articulate. Similarly, although Mrs Shears is the first person to speak, she does so by shouting and swearing at Christopher.

Analysis could focus on the irony that Christopher's inability to understand the subtext of others' language means he has found non-verbal ways to communicate more effectively. Ed's frustration with Christopher suggests that Christopher is communicating poorly but Ed does not express this explicitly even though he tries to soften the tone of what he is saying with 'mate'. In comparison, Mrs Alexander recognises that direct communication is required for greater clarity.

Pages 44–45

Quick Test

1. Family, friends and strangers.
2. Ed kills Wellington because he is angry that Mrs Shears won't have a relationship with him; Christopher leaves home because he discovers the truth about the breakdown in his parents' relationship and so he no longer trusts his father.
3. Ed takes good practical care of Christopher but they do not connect emotionally, partly because this is difficult for Christopher and partly because Ed is keeping secrets.
4. He dreams of living alone as an astronaut in space.

Exam Practice

Answers could acknowledge that although Christopher groups his relationships quite specifically, not everyone in the groups sees themselves in the same way. His groupings can also be quite limited – Siobhan does not fall into any of his categories although in many ways she is the most consistent relationship he has – probably as a way of controlling his anxiety about relating to people.

Analysis might focus on Christopher's negative rejection of people in 'not' and 'no one' in contrast to Ed's emphatic 'I have to' to 'show' him that he can be trusted, presumably because Christopher does not believe what Ed says.

Pages 46–47

1. Christopher's journey of personal growth towards being more self-reliant.
2. The discovery of Wellington and Christopher's decision to solve the murder.
3. Christopher has to overcome a lot of fear and do a lot of things on his own that he has never done before. This is made more difficult by his struggles to communicate with people effectively.
4. Christopher has an increased sense of what he can do and an increased desire to do more ambitious things with his life.

Exam Practice

Answers should include the observation that whilst Christopher does develop a better sense of independence that can be evidenced through the things he starts to say over the course of the play, he will always have Asperger syndrome. Characteristics such as being direct, literal and factual are always likely to be a feature of his language style.

Analysis might comment on the repeated phrase 'I'm going', which tracks Christopher's development from engaging in a murder mystery, a localised hobby that interests him, to the very real task of travelling afar and alone. The verb choice 'starts' shows that Christopher's need to rely on himself is new and the pronoun 'himself' emphasises his isolation in having to do so. The conjunction 'then' projects beyond the immediacy of his current circumstances, a new way of thinking in itself, to a possible new life of his choosing.

Pages 48–49

1. As an astronaut he may get to live alone, which he would like.
2. Christopher's struggle to effectively connect with other people and his distance from them.
3. They do not literally describe what they represent and need interpreting.
4. By using deduction as part of his detection.
5. He uses a spiral to find his way to the train station.

Exam Practice

Analysis could include Christopher's interest in space symbolising his isolation from others, the repetition of 'thousands' emphasising the strength of his need to feel in control of his separation and the definite word 'know' ensuring that such security has been achieved. His logical interpretation of the metaphor is humorous because it is true, exposing the audience to their own lack of sense. 'Therefore' shows he has made his detecting a puzzle by using deduction, although the modal verb 'most' is not definite as he does not yet know it to be true.

Pages 50–51

1. Maths has definite answers. It requires logical thought and problem-solving skills.
2. He finds solace in equations and calms himself down by counting different types of numbers.
3. Ed recognises that Christopher has a significant skill in maths. As well as what a positive outcome would facilitate for Christopher in the future, Ed wants Christopher to feel the personal benefit of being successful as ordinarily there are so many other areas in which he struggles in comparison to others.
4. That he now has both the confidence and the skills to achieve his ambitions.

Exam Practice

Answers should recognise that whereas Christopher is often not as good as others at many things, his abilities in maths far outstrip most people. Through maths, he can feel achievement, rather than feeling diminished, and can use his ability to practical purpose; 'one thing' betrays Ed's frustration at all the other things that Christopher struggles with in contrast to 'good at', which makes the school seem churlish for not allowing him to take the exam. The audience can imagine deeper meaning to Ed feeling 'proud', as the exam is the culmination of all Christopher's efforts and trials in the play. Answers may link Christopher saying he was going to get an A* with saying he does not lie. He does get an A*, just as he finds the killer of Wellington and finds his mother in London after saying he was going to achieve both of these aims.

Pages 52–53

1. He believes that dogs are important too.
2. The puppy is a symbol of a fresh beginning after the chaos instigated by Wellington's death.
3. At times, the police lack patience with Christopher, they swear and assume his behaviour is bad because they don't try to understand him. However, the policeman in the train station does try to find out what is wrong with him and to help him.
4. He hides behind the luggage rack so the policeman believes he has left the train and goes to find him.

Exam Practice

In a world where Christopher is often confused by the things people say and do, he finds solace in the predictability of the police and animals. Animals' needs are constant and they cannot lie so he knows where he stands with them. He feels he can say the same for policemen as they uphold the rule of law, which Christopher can adhere to as a guiding set of principles, and by which they should not lie. Ultimately, however,

Christopher is disappointed by the police whereas he is not disappointed by animals.

Pages 54–55

1. Christopher's way of speaking shows us features of his character.
2. He calls his parents Mother and Father.
3. He is uncommonly direct, which can seem abrupt.
4. People find it hard to believe him and challenge him.

Exam Practice

Answers should emphasise that much of Christopher's speech is linked to his Asperger's. He can articulate his basic needs reasonably well but struggles to understand others' implicit meanings.

Analysis might highlight the alliteration of 'dog' and 'dead' drawing attention to the short statement, which he delivers factually, as well as the detail about the policeman and formal use of his own name. The adverb 'always' shows Christopher's thinking, and language, does not give room for interpretation. The odd phrasing of 'do chatting' separates Christopher from the activity and suggests he sees it as a choice, like doing sport. Alternatively, he might be adopting a superior tone as he sees chatting as non-factual and therefore a waste of time.

Pages 56–57

1. Punctuation such as exclamation marks and ellipses.
2. They start swearing.
3. It's not appropriate in front of a young person and is not fair on Christopher as he does not intend to cause others stress.
4. When asked a question, Christopher answers briefly and literally, which often requires the other person to ask another question to get more information.

Exam Practice

Answers could include frustration with Christopher and impatience when dealing with him or a superior sense of being able to make fun of him or pass personal judgements on him.

Analysis could focus on the metaphoric use of 'monkey' and 'prize specimen', the pronoun in 'look at this' or the rhetorical question 'are you for real?', all of which describe Christopher as non-human in some way. 'Prize specimen' and 'look at this' suggest a superior sense of ownership of discovering his difference as interesting enough to show off to others.

Pages 62–63

Quick Test

1. Understanding of the whole text, specific analysis and terminology, awareness of the relevance of context, a well-structured essay and accurate writing.

2. Planning focusses your thoughts and allows you to produce a well-structured essay.
3. Quotations give you more opportunities to do specific AO2 analysis.

Exam Practice

Ideas might include the following: Christopher's mother diving under the waves in Cornwall suggests a carefree spirit and talking about living in a farmhouse in France suggests a desire to escape her real life; in her letters, she says she is 'not patient' and that she 'had dreams that things would get better'. However, life in London with Roger does not seem ideal. She did try to be honest with Christopher when she left and is devastated that he thought she was dead, but maybe she could have done more to know him in the two years they were apart. Although she still gets stressed, she does start to put Christopher before herself to have a second chance at being his mother.

Pages 66–67 and 72–73

Use the mark scheme below to self-assess your strengths and weaknesses. Work up from the bottom, putting a tick by things you have fully accomplished, a ½ by skills that are in place but need securing and underlining areas which need particular development. The estimated grade boundaries are included so you can assess your progress towards your target grade.

Pages 68–69

1. Understanding of the whole text, specific analysis and terminology, awareness of the relevance of context, a well-structured essay and accurate writing.
2. Planning focusses your thoughts and allows you to produce a well-structured essay.
3. Quotations give you more opportunities to do specific AO2 analysis.

Exam Practice

Ideas might include the following: at the start, the audience believe the Boone family has been a functional unit that suffers by Judy's apparent death; sympathy is created for Ed and Christopher and Ed is respected as a single father. The affair, Judy's departure and Ed's attempted relationship with Mrs Shears suggests that the unit was broken. Ed and Christopher do not have much emotional connection and Christopher does not recognise Judy's absence as a loss. His sickness on discovering that Judy is alive and his journey to find her suggest his need for family connection. The unit is renegotiated on more honest, accepting and genuine terms.

Grade	AO1 (12 marks)	AO2 (12 marks)	AO3 (6 marks)	AO4 (4 marks)
6–7+	A convincing, well-structured essay that answers the question fully. Quotations and references are well chosen and integrated into sentences. The response covers the whole play.	Analysis of the full range of Stephens' methods. Thorough exploration of the effects of these methods. Accurate range of subject terminology.	Exploration is linked to specific aspects of the play's contexts to show a detailed understanding.	Consistent high level of accuracy. Vocabulary and sentences are used to make ideas clear and precise.
4–5	A clear essay that focusses on the exam question. Quotations and references support ideas effectively. The response refers to different points in the play.	Explanation of Stephens' different methods. Clear understanding of the effects of these methods. Accurate use of subject terminology.	References to relevant aspects of context to show a clear understanding.	Good level of accuracy. Vocabulary and sentences help to keep ideas clear.
2–3	The essay has some good ideas that are mostly relevant. Some quotations and references are used to support ideas.	Identification of some different methods used by Stephens to convey meaning. Some subject terminology used.	Some awareness of how ideas in the play link to context.	Reasonable level of accuracy. Errors do not get in the way of the essay making sense.